COUNTRY FLOORS

Decorating with

TILES

COUNTRY FLOORS

Decorating with TILES

Roslyn Siegel ✺ Introduction by Norman Karlson

FRIEDMAN/FAIRFAX
PUBLISHERS

A FRIEDMAN/FAIRFAX BOOK

©1995 by Michael Friedman Publishing Group, Inc.

Library of Congress Cataloging-in-Publication Data available upon request.

ISBN 1-56799-624-8

Editor: Tim Frew
Art Director: Jeff Batzli
Designer: David Shultz
Photography Director: Christopher C. Bain
Photography Editors: Daniella Jo Nilva and Emilya Naymark

Typeset by BPE Graphics, Inc.
Color separations by South Sea International Press, Ltd.
Printed in China by Leefung-Asco Printers Ltd.

For bulk purchases and special sales, please contact:
Friedman/Fairfax Publishers
Attention: Sales Department
15 West 26th Street
New York, NY 10010
212/685-6610 FAX 212/685-1307

Visit our website:
http://www.metrobooks.com

Dedication

To all those who have ever been awed by the possibilities contained in a lump of clay.

Acknowledgments

This is at once the story of decorative ceramic tiles and the story of Country Floors, and nobody knows more about both than the founder of Country Floors, Norman Karlson. His keen enthusiasm, encyclopedic knowledge, and extensive personal library made this book possible. The cheerful help of his wife Shannon and daughter Eliza enabled my research to proceed smoothly and easily. The New York staff provided splendid photographs, patiently answered all of my questions, and offered valuable editorial advice. Special thanks to Caroline Fairley and Esther Kraman for their clear and loving descriptions of how tiles are made and used. Overseeing it all was my editor Tim Frew and photo editor Chris Bain who helped me to skillfully put all the pieces together so that this book, like the tiles it describes, can provide long-lasting pleasure to all that have an eye for beauty.

C O N T E N T S

Introduction

O ver the last twenty-five years, interest in decorated ceramic tiles has turned a lackluster, uninspired business into a vibrant, thriving part of the interior design industry.

In 1962, I was a photographer doing advertising and magazine work. While on holiday in Florence, I passed a small tile shop along the Arno, away from the center of town. This charming, well-stocked shop sold tiles the likes of which I had never seen before in America. I purchased about 500 square feet for use in my house on 26th street in New York City. Before having them installed in my bath, however, I used them as a prop in a photo shoot for *Ladies' Home Journal*. The photo that finally appeared in the magazine was small, but did manage to generate over five-hundred inquiries. Instead of answering all the mail, I immediately searched the city for local sources of tile. What I found was a great void in the North American market.

As the next step, my small studio staff of two sent out mass mailings to every tile maker we could find in Italy, Spain, France, Portugal, and Holland. Then in 1964, after one year of research, I went on my first buying trip to visit the choicest of the factories we had discovered. I came back from that trip having purchased only a few pallets from each company.

The block at 214 East 26th street was never quite the same after that, with large trailer trucks barely fitting in the narrow street and blocking traffic while we unloaded boxes by hand into the small basement. Our first store was the vault basement under the sidewalk of my studio. Today, Country Floors occupies the first three floors of a historic building in New York. We also have showrooms in Los Angeles, Philadelphia, Miami, Sydney, and Melbourne, with representatives in most other major U.S. and Australian cities.

Although tile style has changed and the industry has grown over the years, we still carry some of the first patterns from four of the original artisan factories. Today, we purchase from twenty-five to thirty factories in Europe.

INTRODUCTION

Some are large mass production factories and some are small artisan factories. In the past decade Country Floors has also begun to work with a number of small studios and tile makers in the United States. My wife Shannon and I visit these factories several times a year. Our strongest attachment is always to the smaller artisan factories that produce tiles close to, and sometimes exactly the same as, those they did two or three hundred years ago.

In northern Holland across the Zuider Zee to Friesland is Makkum, the oldest known tile factory in Europe. It is under the direction of Pieter Jan Tichelaar, who is the eighth generation descendant from Freeark Jan Tichelaar, the owner and director in 1674. The family name of "Tichelaar" actually means tile maker in Dutch. I have studied an old pattern book dated 1700 and I found that the drawings were identical to the tiles that are made today, 288 years later. This factory is practically a museum and is visited by almost every Dutch school child and countless numbers of travellers.

Another of our favorite tile makers is in Seville, Spain. He has been inspired by the tiles made originally by the Moors in the fifteenth century. They chipped out geometrical forms and shapes from glazed pieces of tile with a small hammer while holding the tile between their toes. Each artisan could make about two square feet a day. The style remained popular after the Moors left Spain, so the Spanish developed a less tedious process where they used greasy pieces of string to divide the colors. This system was called *cuenca secca*, or dry string.

Another modern advancement made in the sixteenth century was to mold the tile with a fine relief edge to separate the colors in the design. This process is called *cuenca*, or basin. These two systems are still produced today in all of the old patterns by Sr. Francisco M. Rodriques. His old factory was inside Seville; however, because of the growth of Seville in the past decade the factory had to move to a modern, up-to-date plant away from the city. The new plant, with all of its fine, new gas kilns, experimented for two years unsuccessfully trying to reproduce the beautiful copper luster glazes of old. Fortunately, bureaucratic red tape had prevented the old factory from being converted into modern apartments. Sr. Rodriques went back to the site and drew plans from the old underground Arab kiln and carefully recreated it in the backyard of his modern factory. Today, one can again look down through the grates and see a person throwing shovels of olive pits into the fire just as they had always done to produce the most magical copper glaze.

Portugal is the country of tiles: All of its buildings are covered with them. If there is a wall, it is probably covered with a blue and white mural. Many of these tiles date back to 1755 when an earthquake destroyed half of Lisbon and there was a resurgence of tile making to repair and rebuild the city. There are a few factories that still produce tiles exactly as they did over two-hundred years ago.

The tile designs in this book were chosen to provide a broad view of the endless potential of decorative ceramic tile. Many of them combine the old with the new to produce interiors that are beautiful, engaging, and stunningly original.

I hope this book brings to light the wonderful world of ceramic tiles and its vast history. Perhaps you, too, will soon look up at old buildings and tile interiors and marvel at this age-old artisan art form that has changed the face of architecture from ancient Persia to today.

9

TILES YESTERDAY

The Spanish flavor of this enchanting pool (opposite page) is created by the Giralda relief tiles from Spain along one end and the octagon terra cotta tiles that pave the patio floor. Note the dramatic beauty of the glazed inserts among the terra cotta tiles, and how the different shapes, colors, and patterns add excitement to the space.

From the War Chariot of Ramses III, charging across the walls of his tomb, to the great dragon guarding the gates of Babylonia, to the glittering geometrics of Topkapi, to the jewellike pavement of Westminster Abbey, tiles have adorned the ancient and medieval world. Tile making quickly spread to Europe from Egypt, where it began four hundred years before the birth of Christ. Merchants and warriors, Moorish invaders, and Catholic crusaders brought the secret of the shimmering glazes that seemed to capture the sun's rays. From the Iberian peninsula, tiles made their way across the sea to the New World in the baggage of the conquistadores. In the Americas, tiles were seen by Native Americans for the first time in churches, where they were used as decorative elements.

Tiles were used originally to adorn the walls of palaces, temples, and tombs with religious and heraldic symbols. During the Renaissance tilemakers began to depict themes from mythology and even such simple motifs as the pleasures of a country stroll or a shepherd tending his sheep. By the eighteenth century in the Netherlands, tiles had become the delight of the bourgeoisie and were used to face fireplaces and bedrooms walls. Soon they covered the walls of various hard-to-clean shops, such as those of butchers and fishmongers. During the nineteenth century, the Victorians had their portraits done in tile and used the graceful tendrils of Art Nouveau designs to adorn their homes and public buildings. In America, tiles were used to pave the floors of homes and elegant apartment buildings.

The historical worldwide popularity of ceramic tiles is no mystery. Clay, made of kaolin (aluminum silicate) plus quartz or sand and traces of minerals such as mica, feldspar, and iron, is the most plentiful substance on earth. Easy to dig, form, and mold when damp, it can be baked to the toughness of cement. A glaze, which is nothing more than a glass compound colored with metal oxide, chemically bonds with the silica in the clay body when fired. This forms a decorative, durable surface that actually becomes part of the tile itself.

Firing is accomplished in kilns or ovens fueled by wood, gas, electricity, or even olive pits. High- and low-temperature firing can be controlled for different effects. While most decorative ceramic tiles are fired twice or even three times; those decorated with slip (liquid clay) are usually fired just once (biscuit firing).

With advances that produced a variety of color, relief, and transfer techniques, tile work attracts the skill of the painter, potter, sculptor, glass maker, and even photographer. From a practical point of view, it is cheaper and easier to work with than stone but just as long lasting. Since it is easy to keep clean and reflects the light, it has always been particularly favored in sunny climates.

The history of tile making is truly international. The first blue copper glazes and inlaid colored clay came from

Opposite page: *The size and shape of ceramic tiles add architectural interest to this portico.* **Right:** *Tumbled marble from Italy adds old-world warmth and a look of antiquity to this foyer and staircase.*

Egypt and Babylonia. From China came high-fired white tiles, the forerunner of porcelain. From Persia came blue-green glazed sarcophagi and mosaic pavements. Because of its jewellike appearance, the Persians used tile to face the walls of their mosques and to line their prayer niches. In the thirteenth and fourteenth centuries, Persian tile makers perfected a brown lustre glaze and devised a method to paint gold leaf onto the tiles by means of a stencil.

Most of the ceramic techniques that were later used in Europe originated in Persia. Mosaics were first produced by embedding small fragments of glazed clay into a layer of mortar, which was then spread over an outside wall. Later, small pieces of glazed tiles were combined with this treatment to form pictures and designs of great beauty. In addition to their famed geometrics, the Persians depicted delicate birds, graceful scrollwork, and even hunting scenes. Using low-fired enamel paints, they created "minai" or "seven-color" ceramic tiles, of red, white, black, and gold on blue. The Persians found that with tiles they could imitate the shadows and effect of stucco

The Giralda relief tiles from Spain on these two pages reproduce the luster of their Moorish ancestor.

14

walls. They carved designs in high relief, in white, purple, and blue.

For the English during the medieval period, inlaid or "encaustic" tile proved to be a practical yet magnificent paving material. This style consisted of carving a design in red clay tile and filling the depression with a yellow liquid clay (slip). The tile was then covered with a yellowish transparent lead glaze that protected and darkened the colors.

Two other medieval techniques were *sgraffito*, in which a cover of slip was scraped away, exposing a background clay of contrasting color, and raised relief designs, which were produced by pressing wooden blocks into the clay.

Primitive printing techniques were also widely used. A piece of wood with a raised pattern was dipped in slip and then pressed onto the surface of the tile, leaving a pattern much like any inked stamp.

In the fifteenth century, the Turks perfected a type of underglaze painting. Blue, white, and black designs were painted under a transparent glaze. For the first time black and blue designs appeared on a white background, showing the influence of Chinese ceramics. In Istanbul in the sixteenth century, a thick red glaze that stood out like a relief, called sealing-wax red, was created.

The Moors carried their arabesques and geometrics into Granada. At the same time, however, Spanish tile makers were influenced by Italian tile style. About the year 1500, the Italian potter Francisco Niculoso arrived in Seville and introduced the themes of the Renaissance (such as mythological subjects). The best of his gifts was skill in maiolica tiles—painting brightly colored glazes on a white opaque background of tin oxide. The tin oxide glaze solved the problem of running colors that had forced the Spanish to outline their designs either by grooves (*cuerda seca*) or with raised ridges (*de cuenca*). The tin glaze (a transparent lead glaze to which tin is added to make a white, opaque glaze) fixed the other colors, which were painted on top. Copper oxide was used to make green, manganese compound for violet and black, aniline compound for yellow, iron compound for red, and cobalt for blue.

The burnished colors are a result of firing underground in wood-burning kilns.

In Italy tile making was considered a high art during the Renaissance, sharing in the imagination and feeling found in paintings of the period. In Faenza, a flawless, glasslike transparent glaze was produced that led to international renown. In Sienna, a pure black glaze was developed that provided a sculptured quality to portraits.

French tiles of this period favored engravings of marine subjects—yellow with a blue background. The wavelike or striped patterns representing the sea were distinctive.

Portugal, however, showed the most fondness for tiles. Before the earthquakes of 1755 destroyed many of the buildings in Lisbon, ninety percent of its churches and monasteries and seventy-five percent of its old mansions were adorned or faced with decorative ceramic tile in the Spanish style. After 1755, checkerboard patterns of monotonal tiles in blue, green, white, and yellow made their appearance.

This fireplace (opposite page) *lends color and pattern to the room. These brilliant blue and yellow border tiles* (left) *liven up a kitchen.*

The fame of Italian tile spread into the Netherlands. In the sixteenth century, Guido di Savino came to Antwerp to start a whole new industry, bringing with him bright colors painted on a white tin glaze. Savino also perfected the "reserving" technique used extensively on the walls and pavements of Antwerp. In this technique an outline was drawn and the background painted in, creating a white pattern on a dark background.

At the same time the Dutch began producing tiles in large numbers. These tiles, while not innovative in technique, have won acclaim for their realism and humor. While in many of the countries of Europe, tiles were strictly for the aristocrats, here the middle class culture made its mark. Children playing, jugglers, peasants, country landscapes, and expressions of middle class folklore and sentiments found their way onto decorative tile. The Dutch often employed *trompe l'oeil* techniques and produced large scale decorative effects by alternating white tiles with decorated ones. Facing fireplaces with decora-

tive brick had always been a speciality of the Netherlands since in the Middle Ages homes were still made of wood. Early decorations were made by stamping a design into the clay. Beautiful faience tiles took the place of these decorative bricks in the sixteenth century and formed

These picture tiles of country landscapes (opposite page) provide a rustic focal point to this otherwise modern kitchen. Royal Makkum picture tiles from Holland have a tradition of representing scenes from everyday life.

links between the tiles of southern Europe, Asia, and northern Europe. Ceramic house signs announced shops and trades. They were used behind beds, on winding staircases, along window frames, and in cellars and passageways.

Dutch Royal Makkum tiles recreate the scenes that made delftware world famous. Note the decorative border that is used as a framing device.

In the eighteenth century, delftware became widely accepted because of the rise of the middle class. These tiles were influenced by Chinese porcelain, many showing Chinese figures in oriental landscapes. Delftware tiles were often distinguished by a framing device—a circle, hexagon, or other decorative border. Pinhole indentations at each corner, a result of having been fastened to the cutting board during production, were characteristically present.

Many of the typical delft designs were painted by a method called "pouncing" in which the design was pricked out on a paper. Charcoal dust was then rubbed over the paper leaving an outline on the tile, which was then painted in by hand. These tiles were sometimes fired three times to accommodate certain colors that would not survive the high-temperature of the second firing.

The Dutch delftware was so popular that it was also produced in England; however, the English delft blue-

This Pastorale mural is made of tiles from France. French murals can be made up from as few as three tiles to as many as fifty-five.

© Phillip Ennis

Transfer painting enabled craftsmen to create intricate designs such as these (left and far right) on the surface of tiles. This kitchen (right) uses a modern-day version of the English transfer tiles.

tinged glaze suffered in comparison with the pure white of the Dutch. In Liverpool, England during the 1750s, John Sandler and Guy Green invented transfer painting, an innovation that would revolutionize tile making. This process involved printing designs from wood blocks or copper plates on thin paper using oiled ceramic color as ink. The printed paper would then be placed ink-side down on the tile, rubbed firmly, and then soaked off, leaving the ink design within the glaze. This technique of transfer painting greatly facilitated production of decorated tiles. In an affidavit dated July 27, 1756, Sandler and Green swore that they, "without the aid or assistance of any other person or persons, did within the space of six hours, to wit, between the hours of nine in the morning and three in the afternoon of the same day, print upwards of twelve hundred Earthenware tiles of different patterns, at Liverpoole, aforesaid, and which, as these deponents have heard and believe, were more in number and better and neater than one hundred skillful pot-painters could have painted in the like space of time."

With this technique it now became possible to reproduce both paints and the fine lines found in etchings. Complicated designs, elaborately dressed figures in the French style, depictions of Aesop's Fables, and portraits of actors

and actresses from the English theater found their way onto English ceramic tiles.

Another English innovation—dust-pressed tiles, tiles made from powdered clay, invented by Richard Prosser and patented in 1840 by Herbert Minton—raised tile making to yet another level. Now the tiles exhibited less shrinkage and could be made thinner and smoother. This method could produce up to eighteen hundred six-inch tiles a day. Pressing machines were hand operated until 1873, when Maw and Co. made the first steam-driven press. Molded tiles were manufactured by using a metal or plaster die in the dust-pressing process.

The Victorians updated the ancient traditions and adapted the modern ones. Their tiles demonstrated hand painting, slip painting, tube lining, sgraffito, transfer print-ing, molding, inlay, and aerography. Slip decoration employed liquid clay of varying colors for decorate effects. It was applied to unfired clay, then fired, glazed clear, and fired again. Tube lining piped slip around the edges of a drawing. A translucent glaze could be poured between the raised lines before or after the first firing.

The Victorian transfer prints were applied on biscuit-fired clay, then glazed, to protect the decoration. This differed from Sandler's original method in which prints were applied on top of glaze. Transfer printing was made easier by F.W.M. Collins and Alfred Reynolds in 1848, who used stone or zinc plates instead of copper. Now, several flat areas of color could be produced by making several consecutive impressions on the same piece of paper.

Minton and Maw revived the medieval inlaid or encaustic tile technique in the nineteenth century and produced patterns of many different-colored clays. Dust-pressed encaustic tiles could also make pseudo-mosaic patterns, tiles with pressed ridges that looked like mosaic patterns. Aerography was accomplished with a stencil over tiles and ceramic color blown on with an airbrush or sprayed on. Color applied in this manner can be detected by stipples or specks in the color field. Hand painting can usually be distinguished from all other techniques by its bold, free strokes.

Like their variety of techniques, the themes of the Victorian designers were wide-ranging—tile makers favored naturalism, flowers, birds, landscapes, classical myths, oriental landscapes, and Japanese woodblock designs. William Morris, of the Arts and Crafts Movement, whose works were exhibited at the Great Exhibition at the Crystal Palace in 1851, revised the stylized, simple, flat designs and bold lines from Japan and Persia. Designs like these were also favored by William De Morgan. De Morgan experimented with luster painting, using a compound with a metallic oxide on the surface of the tile. When smoke was introduced into the kiln, the oxide would change to a thin film of metal, giving luster to the tile. The Art Nouveau style, influenced strongly by Aubrey Beardsley, exhibited a preference for freedom of design—delicate tendrils that entwined and meandered all over the tile.

With Herbert Minton, Collins and Reynolds patented the lithographic transfer of design that enabled them to produce even more elaborate designs—illustrations of Tennyson's poems and scenes from novels by Sir Walter Scott.

In America, the first native tiles, suitably enough, depicted the American flag. They were made in the 1850s in Bennington, Vermont for the Crystal Palace Exhibition in New York. In the 1870s, the Low Art Tile Company produced glazed relief tiles called "Natural Tiles" in which a real leaf or stem was impressed in the wet clay and glazed with transparent glaze in one color.

An innovative process was developed by The American Encaustic Tile Company in Ohio. It produced relief tiles in the 1870s with portraits that looked like photos. Their secret was a black translucent glaze that covered the

© Phillip Ennis

Note how the directional lines of the wall tiles and the floor tiles create a pattern of contrasting grids.

These antique floral tiles were made using English transfer techniques.

portrait, its varying thickness giving it different tones of gray, simulating black and white photographs. The Rookwood Pottery in Cincinnati in the 1880s brought tile production back in touch with its artistic, rather than its commercial, roots by hiring graduates of local art schools to paint its tiles.

The tile industry prospered from the mid-nineteenth century until the middle of the twentieth, when the competition from wallpaper seemed to drive many firms out of business. In the 1980s and 1990s, we have experienced a tile renaissance as people have become concerned once more with beautiful, long-lasting natural materials.

TILES TODAY

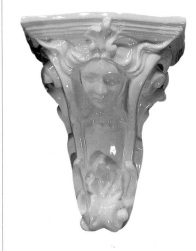

oday, tiles are produced in many of the same countries that have been producing them since the medieval period, with a few newcomers. Italy leads the world in tile production, followed by such countries as Spain, Holland, France, England, Germany, Japan, Portugal, Morocco, and the United States. Turkey and Iran, which once were major tile producers, now have a limited output.

America, during the Arts and Crafts Movement from 1865–1930, was one of the largest tile producers in the world, with the biggest factories in Ohio, New Jersey, and Pennsylvania. Today many small tile producers, which are part of the legacy of the crafts movement of the sixties, operate a number of factories throughout the country. As a direct result of their association with Country Floors, these small tile manufacturers have been able to survive and expand. Tuned in to contemporary lifestyles and fashion trends, these factories are producing uniquely American patterns and designs.

Japan, a newcomer to the field with no native tile industry, is catching up quickly with mass-produced decorative tiles. Mexico continues to produce numbers of inexpensive tiles whose rustic, irregular look lends a special flavor to country design.

Today's tile makers use an arsenal of techniques handed down by medieval, Renaissance, and Victorian tile makers. One small factory in Seville, Spain, learned the hard way that modern techniques are not necessarily

White handcrafted and incised tiles with a touch of pattern and texture provide visual interest without overwhelming the space.

better. Accustomed to firing its kilns with olive pits, this factory decided to invest in a modern electrical system, only to discover that the glaze lacked its usual depth and glow. The company quickly went back to olive pits.

Most factories that make decorative tiles—that is, any tile that is not a solid color—use a combination of hand-painting and mechanical techniques. Certain tiles are made especially for the floor and others for the wall, and they generally are not interchangeable. There is good reason for this. Interior wall tiles tend to be thinner and their glazes cannot withstand the abrasive effect of constant foot travel. If set correctly, however, tiles are among the most enduring building materials—they can last for hundreds of years.

Today's tile makers have learned how to improve the durability of materials so there is a group of painted tiles for the floors. Many tiles have been made acid-proof for use on kitchen countertops. Durability is somewhat predictable: Country Floors offers a guide for those tiles best suited for light stress, moderate stress, normal stress, and commercial stress. Certain tiles have proven themselves for entryways and halls, others for balconies, terraces, and patios.

Designs have traditionally been based on geometrics, florals, pastoral scenes, birds, animals, fruits, and vegetables. Tile design now follows the trends in painting, textiles, and interior decoration, transforming the traditional designs and patterns. Pastel pinks, turquoise blues, pale

greens, and lavenders now make their appearance. The grays, roses, purples, and greens popular in the twenties, thirties, and forties have reappeared, updating the familiar geometric patterns, composed of interlocking circles, stars, squares, and hexagons. Metallics have become popular with copper, gold, and silver glittering against a dark or even black background.

Contemporary designs often rely upon influences from the past. Various themes and patterns have been revived, combined, or altered to suit modern living spaces. In many designs for which this is the case, the historical origins are evident even though the scale and color have been altered. Young designers such as Nino Caruso have made a name for themselves by creating tile patterns in just this way. Others have found success basing designs on the paintings of Picasso and other well-known artists.

To a large extent, the popularity of tiles in this country is due to Norman Karlson, founder/owner of Country Floors. He was the first to gather tiles from all over the world and bring them to the United States, Australia, and Canada.

© Phillip Ennis; Interior Design by Susan Kelly

Opposite page: The simplicity of the solid-color tile balances the ornate beauty of the Giralda Spanish tiles. Center: Blank tiles interspersed with picture tiles create a gentle rhythm that provides interest without overwhelming the space. The delicacy of these picture tiles set against a white background make them perfect candidates for mix and match design.

The combination of terra cotta and decorative glazed tiles gives this staircase (right) *a totally different look from the top than from the bottom. An inset of tiles framing a fireplace* (far right) *enhances the warmth of the room. Note how it complements the wood.*

He has made these tiles both familiar and, perhaps most important, accessible.

In 1962 he returned from a trip to Italy with a few painted tiles that had caught his eye. He spread them out on the floor of his kitchen for a photograph that appeared in *Ladies Home Journal* that same year. The five hundred letters he received asking for information about the availability of these tiles led him to discover that there was no availability. The only way one could buy these tiles was to take a trip to Italy.

Between 1964, when Norman Karlson founded Country Floors in the basement of his photographic studio, and the present, Karlson made hundreds of trips, not only to Italian factories, but to factories all over the world. Locating small workshops of artisans, or *ateliers*, rather than factories, Karlson collaborated with the craftsmen, encouraging them to reproduced authentic designs found in museums all over Europe. In consultation with the curators of these museums, he searched their archives for patterns he felt needed resurrection or preservation. Often a simple change of color, the addition of a new graphic element (or the dropping of another), resulted in a highly successful, contemporary design.

Today, many European factories use Country Floors as the exclusive importer of their designs to the United States, Canada, and Australia. Country Floors has been honored by such organizations as the Association of Italian Tile Manufacturers for its marketing success and its contributions to the enhancement of the tile industry's overall image.

THE ELEMENTS OF STYLE

No matter how many reasons there may be for the enormous popularity of tiles throughout history—plentiful clay, endurance, ease of maintenance—the real truth is that people like them simply because they are beautiful. Tiles have the ability to transform an ordinary room into something extraordinary by enhancing even the dullest surface with glowing color, pattern, and texture.

The enormous range of tiles available today suggests some fascinating variations on the basic decorating traditions that have been handed down from the Renaissance. Traditional tiles can be combined in nontraditional patterns, and old designs can be mixed with new ideas for something unique and current.

But having so many tiles to choose from can pose another problem. How do you decide which colors, textures, sizes, and shapes are best suited to your decorating needs? Your decision will depend partly on your decorating goal and partly on your own style preferences.

First, ask yourself what you want the tiles to do for your home. Do you want them to create a dramatic center in the room or to serve as a backdrop for your furniture and fabrics? Do you want them to disguise an awkward element in the room or emphasize an architectural ornament? Do you want them to increase the sense of space in an area, or to diminish it? Is your goal to unify disparate areas, or to delineate sections of a

cumbersome space? Do you want them to emphasize the horizontal or the vertical, to lower the ceiling or raise it?

Next, look at the overall interior design of your apartment or house. Does it have a sleek, modern look? A French country motif? If your interior design has an overall theme or style, you may want to mirror that in your tiling project. An ornate Victorian bathroom may be beautiful; however, when installed in an otherwise Memphis-oriented apartment, the contrast may be too jarring. It is important to remember, however, that there are no hard and fast rules when it comes to tile design or interior design in general. Some of the most pleasing results can come from the most unusual combinations.

The overall feeling of a room decorated in tiles is the result of several elements: color, pattern, size, shape, and texture. The success of any tiling project comes from consolidating these elements into a coherent, well-executed design scheme.

Left: *Several different patterns are combined here for an opulent effect. The repetition of color unifies the overall design.* Right: *Contemporary art tiles from Portland, Oregon, provide just the right touch of color and pattern for this contemporary kitchen.*

© Charles S. White; Interior Design by Barbara Windom

© Barbara Mundall

COLOR

While tiles are made in virtually every color imaginable, the most traditional tile colors are blue and white. This is a direct result of the traditional popularity of delft tiles and ancient Chinese pottery. On the other hand, the Spanish and the Portuguese loved vibrant colors, and today, royal blue is often combined with yellow and orange.

Over the past two-hundred years, the popularity of tiles has been greatly affected by fashion, with the colors of the tiles reflecting whatever colors were in vogue at the time. The Art Nouveau period made use of pale green, vivid purple, and pink; the Art Deco period favored orange, maroon, and turquoise; the forties featured the off-shades of pink-purple, brown-maroon, and yellow-green. The sixties favored the earth colors of almond, beige, and rust, while the seventies liked the sparse, clean look of white and black. In the eighties there was a move toward pastels, and in the nineties we have seen subtle changes in the neutral palette and the advent of more saturated colors.

No matter what fashion dictates, however, pure white tiles have always remained among the most popular and versatile of all. They are equally as attractive in the traditional country home as they are in the contemporary city apartment. White rectangular tiles, when used in a brick pattern, provide a Victorian or antique look. When arranged vertically, they create a hi-tech and modern look. A white-on-white relief tile lends a touch of old-world elegance—the look of lace—while a handmade white tile provides a hint of the rustic. Used with a border in a solid accent color or design, white tile can provide virtually any look at all. Perhaps one of the most effective uses of white is when it is interspersed with other single-color tiles. The contrasting ability of white can bring even the most muted color alive. Among the most versatile color mixers are blue and green. Classic combinations for kitchens and bathrooms include blue with white and green with white.

Two other extremely popular colors are salmon and peach. These soft, gentle colors are particularly popular

© Charles S. White; Barbara Windom, interior design

Left: *The vibrant mixture of royal blue and vivid yellow in this kitchen shows the direct influence of the Portuguese love of bright colors. Above: Colors such as beige, peach, salmon, and yellow are very popular in bathrooms because they flatter skin tones. The tumbled marble used in this bathroom provides a natural color scheme.*

for bathrooms because they are extremely easy on the eye. Gray and beige also make excellent decorating colors. They blend well with both bright, vibrant colors and pale tones alike.

Choosing a color scheme depends on a number of factors: the colors you like best, the colors already in or near the room, the feeling you hope to convey, and probably some of the color preferences you have absorbed from the current fashion trends. In fact, fashion plays such a great role in choosing tile color that designers say they can often tell customers' favorite colors by what they wear to the showroom. Chances are these favorite colors are already present in the furnishings at home.

If, somehow, none of the hundreds of colors already available are completely satisfying, a new color can be custom ordered. Colors can also be matched with fabrics to create a coordinated environment for each room.

This blue and white combination (left) gets an extra lift from the solid blue corner tiles that frame the tub and create a wainscotting effect along the walls. This border (above) nicely frames the mirror. Gray tiles wake up with this splashy border design (right).

Color is arguably the most multifaceted decorating element in any room. Certain color combinations suggest feelings and attitudes that are almost universal. Black and white convey a hi-tech, modern look, while pink and yellow evoke a more delicate, romantic feeling. Combining pale colors provides a restful effect. Sharp contrasts, such as black and gold, and red and midnight blue, work to create drama. Unusual color combinations—lilac and red, pink and green—can be exciting and unsettling, a focal point in the room. Almost any color combination can look good if the two components are of similar tone and value.

The method in which glaze color is applied can also create a difference in feeling. Machine-made tiles look more precise; their glaze is often uniform and sharp. Handmade tiles look quite different. Their glaze is not uniform and so the light hits the surface at uneven angles, creating a more rustic, informal look.

Understanding the science of color can help you to create interesting special effects. Colors, in general, change in appearance according to their arrangement. A dark color placed near a lighter color will appear deeper, while the lighter color will appear brighter, accentuating the contrast between them. For example, when situated next to blue, red will appear a bit more yellow, but when the same red is placed next to yellow it will appear more blue. Glossy black walls provide an especially high intensity backdrop for any contrasting color.

The size and shape of the space you are working with is another important factor that will figure into your choice of a color theme. If you look at every space with a critical eye, you will note that each area has its own configuration and its own advantages and limitations. Color can work to your benefit in enhancing the advantages and in minimizing or disguising the limitations.

This delicate floral, used only part way up the wall, lends a traditional touch to the space while serving as a backdrop for antique furnishings. These Rochelle hand-painted faience tiles from France have the light, airy feel of a water color. Their antique look derives from designs that originated in the fourteenth century.

Strong, dark colors tend to make a large space look smaller and more intimate. Deep reds, greens, browns, and blues can enclose an island kitchen in an open loft space or turn a large, old-fashioned bathroom into a cozy, romantic spa. Sharply contrasting colors are good for adding interest to a room that has fairly regular contours and furnishings that are not too busy. If room fabrics tend to be neutral, most color combinations will work. Unconventional combinations such as green and blue, red and purple, or purple and green will create a more dramatic impact as opposed to the more traditional effect of the classic blue and white.

© Derrick & Love; Interior Design by Robert Schwagerl

Dark colors make this large bathroom (left) seem warm and intimate, while white makes this small bathroom (right) appear larger.

On the other hand, if you have a small or narrow space, pale colors make the walls seem to recede. White is particularly useful for camouflaging irregular shapes and proportions. If you have a bathroom carved out under the roof or a kitchen squeezed into a subdivided apartment, white tiles can conceal boxed-in pipes and unusual angles.

Solid-color and low-contrast schemes are also extremely useful in oddly-shaped spaces and in spaces where the furniture and other features provide the prominent focal points. These color schemes tend to normalize the unusual, while blending into the overall interior design. They can be just as effective as high-contrast schemes; however, they do their work in a more subtle, unobtrusive way.

PATTERN

Color and pattern go hand-in-hand in creating mood. Perhaps the most important idea to keep in mind is not which pattern you choose, but how you choose to distribute that pattern in the space you have. The look you want to achieve will ultimately dictate how you use the pattern.

A large pattern, by its very nature, is going to be more of a feature in a room than a small pattern. However, depending on how it is used and where it is placed, a large pattern can either be played up to act as a focal point or toned down to act as an accent or highlight. For example, a tile mural featuring a luxuriant floral bouquet on a dining room wall will create a dramatic center of visual excitement. The same bold pattern, however, can be used as an accent in the bathroom, serving as a decorative base for the sink or a frame for the mirror.

On the other hand, small patterns, when used all over the room, form a texture that is soothing to the eye and does not call attention to the room itself. This use of pattern allows other objects—a desk, an antique dining table, a grand piano—to act as the focal points of the room. Used in combination with solid colored tiles, a small pattern can also serve as a subtle but effective accent. For example, tile patterns can be used to circle a sink, frame a window, or embellish a kitchen island.

Pattern, both lavish and simple, can be used either to highlight or isolate an element in a room, or as a unifying factor, bringing all of the elements of a room together. It can, for example, create a comfortable niche, carving out a small personal space in a large room. How exciting a simple desk and a dark corner can become if the wall is faced with a dainty Victorian print or a bold geometric design. A rather ordinary window can be transformed into the threshold of a gorgeous garden if it is surrounded by bold floral bouquets, or draped in delicate green vines. An intimate corner in a boudoir, a window seat in a den, or a fruit-laden counter in a breakfast room can be brought to life by the color, pattern, and texture of ceramic tiles.

© Phillip Ennis; Interior Design by Susan Kelly

A combination of blanks, picture tiles, and border tiles transforms these rather ordinary windows into a showcase for beauty. The jars on the windowsill are perfect accents to the installation.

As a unifying theme, pattern can connect rooms with related functions, drawing together what architecture has moved apart. For example, a common border of printed tiles between a kitchen and a family room will visually link these two areas. A baby's bath can be connected to the playroom by complementing patterns, a hallway becomes truly welcoming when it is joined to the entranceway by identical hand-painted tiles.

While to some extent tile design does reflect the taste of the times, it is also an architectural element that has been used for hundreds of years. Many of the patterns—particularly the bold European florals, geometrics, and pictures—have been in production for four hundred years, some made by the same factories, and even the same families, for generations. As a result of the continuation of these time-honored patterns, tiles can provide an historical or a traditional quality even to a newly built home.

PICTURE TILES

Picture tiles have charm and versatility that have been extremely popular throughout the history of tiles. Made in Holland, Portugal, Spain, and France, each tile features a complete picture. The themes include such diverse subjects as Dutch windmills, seascapes, musicians, flowers, children, historic coats of arms, and oriental figures.

Combined with unadorned tiles, these picture tiles can be assembled in different patterns in order to create a truly custom look. Depending on how many are used and how they are arranged, the effect can be dramatic, romantic, traditional, or casual. The corner motif (a small design situated in each of the four corners of the tiles) forms the decorative link from tile to tile, giving unity to the whole design scheme.

Far left: Just a few of these magnificently executed La Rochelle faience tiles from France go a long way towards lending provincial beauty to your home. They represent the evolution of the designs of master potter Cesar Boulongne originating in the fourteenth century (see detail, left) and are examples of some of the finest hand-painting on ceramics. Cuisiniere kitchen wall tiles from Spain (center) combine pictures of fruits and vegetables in a mouth-watering display. Note the decorative tag tiles, which give a particularly French flavor to the design.

MURALS

Murals consist of several tiles that fit together like pieces of a puzzle to complete a particular motif or scene. Once used to decorate the walls of palaces and great houses, murals today are often used to transform entrance foyers, kitchens, and dining rooms into elegant entertaining spaces. They vary in size and shape from a red parrot made up of six tiles, to elaborate French floral designs made up of fifty-five tiles. Other murals can be created by grouping single picture tiles together and setting them off with a border of decorative trim.

Murals are like large elaborate paintings hung on the wall. They can also be used to create *trompe l'oeil* effects. These murals can create interesting architectural elements, such as relief moldings, painted columns, and friezes, in a room where none existed before. The almost endless variations of pictures and tile murals provide a new dimension in decorating.

Left: *Murals from Spain and France consist of sets of tiles ranging from three to an entire wall.* Above: *This charming pair of parrots (upper right) from Spain gives snackers at the breakfast bar something lovely to look at.*

Right: *Made of just six tiles, this parrot can be part of a larger mural consisting of a cockatoo, a vase of sunflowers, and a panel of grapes.*
Far right: *In this custom mural hand-painted by the Tile Guild, birds and flowers adorn* trompe l'oeil *columns, lending an air of elegance to this bathroom.*

51

MIXING TILES

Whether your taste is traditional or contemporary you will discover suitable tile arrangements by mixing tiles. Using a patterned tile within a grouping of solid-colored tiles provides a custom look for any room.

Mixing different kinds of tiles can create a rhythm of color and pattern. Depending upon the intervals of solid color and pattern, the rhythm can be either exciting or restful. Like chords in a musical composition, splashes of pattern will create drama, while single-color tiles suggest calm. An irregular, unexpected combination of patterned with plain tiles will create more interest than a regularly repeated grouping.

Stripes, solids, and grids can be combined to create multiple designs that emphasize the horizontal or vertical space of a room.

THE ELEMENTS OF STYLE

Opposite page, left: *The pale blue and white of these tiles combine with the regularity of the grid pattern to give this contemporary bath a calm and restful ambiance.* Opposite page, right: *This small bath gains height from the vertical lines of the tiles and width from the border tiles that cut the wall in two.* Left: *Verde tumbled marble and relief moldings distinguish the areas of this bathroom from one another through the use of frames and borders.*

BORDERS AND MOLDINGS

In addition to pattern, picture, and mural tiles, there are multiple possibilities offered by borders and moldings. On the very simplest level, patterned borders can be combined with solid-colored tiles: Geometric, ribbon, and rope designs, wisteria, vines, trellis, stripes, dots, and fruit all work well on borders and moldings.

By matching solid-colored tiles or counterpart prints (for example, a grape border surrounding fruit and vegetable tiles) or surrounding full picture or mural tiles with solid-color molding, a designer can create an effective and interesting border that complements and fulfills the overall tile design. Decorated corner tiles and tag tiles—the printed names of spices, food, and wine—can create a European touch when used as borders. Plain white tiles can be dressed up by a bright, floral trim; busy prints can be confined by straight, single-colored borders.

Borders also work well as directional lines that lead the eye across space or from one point of interest to another. They can frame elements in a room or create architectural elements that the room does not have. Of special interest are the three-dimensional, single-colored borders that are reminiscent of hand-carved moldings. These can be especially useful in creating a nineteenth-century look or providing a quiet touch of elegance.

In these tiles from Spain, the rope moldings and floral wave borders define the areas of terra cotta and white-glazed tiles.

PATTERN AND EFFECT

Like color, pattern can be used as a tool to create illusions of space and shape. A pattern on a light background gives the feeling of depth. It helps push back the walls of a small room or make the floor appear wider and longer. Patterns on a dark background tend to enclose a space. Use these to create a sense of intimacy in a study area or powder room.

Patterns with strong geometric or directional lines create the effect of extending space. In particular, a diagonal stripe running across the floor and/or wall will make a room look larger. Width and length can be accentuated by setting tiles at an angle, as the eye will be drawn by geometric lines in any direction.

Pattern can also be used to break up space and to create a three-dimensional effect in a room. Set off an island kitchen by tiling the floor beneath it. Bring down a high ceiling by setting a border of decorative tiles several feet below on the walls. Emphasize the vertical or the horizontal by tiling only one wall in that direction.

Period effects can also be created by pattern. Classic motifs like the egg-and-dart, the acanthus leaf, the Greek key, and the fleur-de-lis draw on a traditional look; a stylized tulip or scallop motif evokes the Art Nouveau period, and a bold chevron design, the Italian modern.

Deciding on how much and what kind of pattern to use will depend on the specifics of each tiling project. If the pattern's function is to accent and emphasize a certain feature in the room—surround a window, enhance a sink, or dramatize an entrance—concentrate the pattern around those elements. If, however, the pattern is meant to enhance the room as a whole or to unify one part of the house with another, distribute it more thoroughly.

Left: In this bathroom scheme inspired by the Arts and Crafts movement, Craftsman tiles with acorn, pine-cone, branch, snail, and tree frog motifs are combined to create a woodsy look that's equally appropriate in a city apartment's kitchen or bath and on a fireplace at a vacation retreat. Right: These glazed and unglazed tiles complement the Mediterranean style of the door, becoming an integrated architectural element of the facade.

SIZE, SHAPE, AND TEXTURE

Hand-painted and solid-colored tiles are important in setting the look and feel of a room as well as establishing its overall scheme. Pattern can be created by size, shape, and texture, which in turn affect the look and feeling of the design. Again, there are no hard and fast rules about which size, shape, or texture of tiles to use in any specific room. It is not true that small rooms need small tiles. On the contrary, it is probably more true that small rooms benefit from larger pieces of tile. The smaller the tile, the more grout lines there will be; the more grout lines, the busier the pattern. Many small rooms may look better with larger tiles that do not visually break up the space into small segments. Many designers recommend mixing sizes for a more interesting effect. From a practical point of view, it is better to use one size for the wall and another for the floor, because unless the house is absolutely perfect, with no settling of foundation, the two tiles will not line up straight.

The standard American tile used to be a simple four-and-a-quarter-inch square. European tile ranges in size— six-, eight-, and twelve-inch squares are standard. Giving the eye a new set of dimensions to look at is always an interesting challenge. The square tile is, however, the most traditional shape around the world. When you change to another shape, the eye will notice it. If you mix shapes and sizes, the tiles will call attention to themselves—the viewer's eye will quickly pick out the elements that are different. The mixing of different sizes and shapes should therefore be done with the discretion of an expert eye.

This border of smaller tiles introduces an element of the unexpected in the shower.

In this bathroom, hand-painted tiles from **Spain** are mixed with tumbled marble from **Italy** and rustic moldings and glazed tile from **California**.

If you decide to play with size and shape, the possibilities are very exciting. For example, terra cotta tiles can be set in different directions for different effects: set on a diagonal for a rustic look, end-to-end for a modern look, and a diamond pattern for something Mediterranean. In the shape of octagons or hexagons, alone or mixed with different sizes and shapes, and even different tiles, terra cotta flooring is the most versatile of all the tile floors.

Solid-colored tiles, in particular, lend themselves to a mixing of shape and size. A combination of triangular tiles, rectangular tiles, and square tiles of different sizes can be pieced together like a puzzle, creating a surface of an intricate deco design or a rhythm of movement resulting from the directional lines formed by the tiles' edges. Floors of rooms can be unified but demarcated by simply shifting a tile from right angles to the diagonal.

Of course, different patterns, colors, and shapes can be mixed together for unique visual effects. In this blue and off white bath, two completely unrelated sets of tiles, both

solid-colors, create an unusual effect primarily by contrasting angles. This outdoor patio and staircase depends on a similar effect for its visual interest: The contrast lies between the small, glazed, black and white checkerboard design of the staircase and the more subtle unglazed, solid-color effect of the terra cotta on the patio.

These Giralda relief tiles (left) add color and depth to the patio wall. The subtle coloration here (right) is a result of hand-dipped glaze on a hand-molded tile, causing light to reflect in unique, distinctive ways.

Pattern and surface interest can be even further enhanced by texture. A group of relief wall tiles from Spain are strongly Moorish in feel, the surface cut by elaborate designs in three dimensions. These tiles, which afford a great deal of pattern in a small area, are particularly impressive outdoors for patios, fountains, and solariums; their cut surfaces reflect light and shadow in an intriguing manner. In this outdoor patio, the relief tiles surrounding the wading pool echo the pool's shape, bringing an Oriental flavor to the setting. The unglazed terra cotta tiles, contrasted with their insets of glazed cobalt blue, defuse the color of the water throughout the patio, connecting all the elements while providing variety and visual interest.

Surface texture, however, can often be more subtle than relief carving in three dimensions. There is, for example, an enormous difference between the texture and feel of hand-made tiles and factory-made tiles. Terra cotta tiles range from the very rustic to the precise. Those from Mexico are irregular in shape and color. Made by hand, they have a rough, intimate quality that some people highly value.

Handmade and hand-glazed tiles have a different surface interest and texture than machine-made tiles. Often, the glaze is unevenly applied. Therefore, each tile will be slightly different in color and shape, making the overall appearance quite different from the crisp uniformity of machine-made tiles.

This surface difference is immediately apparent, particularly among solid-colored tiles. On some, the actual brush strokes are recognizable; on others, the gradations of color appear different in each tile.

The Giralda relief tiles are unmatched in their ability to convey the excitement of color, pattern, and texture, while the Giralda solid-color tiles have a distinctive burnished appearance that gives them a coppery tone.

SIZE, SHAPE, TEXTURE, AND EFFECT

Size, shape, and texture are especially good in creating illusions of space. Tiles with a shiny glaze create a more expanded sense of space than those with a matte glaze. In particular, shiny black tile gives enormous intensity to any color used with it. Mixing different textures can give the illusion of depth and richness, even if the colors are muted. Think of a combination of unglazed terra cotta tiles on the ground contrasted with ornate glazed tiles surrounding a stairwell or swimming pool. Shiny tiles can be used to brighten rooms that don't get much light, matte tiles to create a sense of warmth and coziness.

Use shiny, smooth tiles to camouflage unpleasant angles or proportions of a room. Tiling one wall with a brilliant finish can extend the size of a room, while doing the same with matte tile can make the walls draw closer.

Each element—color, pattern, size, shape, and texture—helps contribute to a total look in an environment. Ideally, they all work together for the same purpose.

Left: The quiet geometry of the floor tiles is a restful complement to the curved excitement of the fountain and its facing tiles. Above: The black background to this picture panel draws the eye as if to a valuable painting. Right: These brightly colored tiles cheer up an interior staircase that gets little natural light.

TILE STYLE

A contrasting border can frame important elements in a room. The border in this bathroom (opposite page) draws attention to the mirror and creates a trompe l'oeil effect on the floor.

After you have considered the endless possibilities in the use of color, pattern, texture, size, and shape, it is time to put all of these elements together in a unified, well-planned tile design. Begin with an overview of the space you will be decorating. Take note of the peculiarities and characteristics of the room. Are there odd angles? What permanent fixtures do you have to contend with in the room? What is the overall shape and size of the room?

Tiles have a unique ability to manipulate the way space is perceived, to emphasize the horizontal or the vertical, and to add or subtract height, width, and depth in any area. Since they come in different colors, patterns, textures, shapes, and sizes, tiles can be tailored to provide an appropriate interior to virtually any room, while solving a multitude of decorating problems.

Use tiles to create new architectural elements in a room. Today, most houses and apartments do not contain many of the decorative architectural touches of yesteryear—fan-shaped windows, carved moldings, wainscoting, and elaborate mantelpieces. Instead, square, utilitarian rooms and windowless baths often characterize the modern home. However, tile as architecture can help re-create the effects of many of these traditional features. For example, three-dimensional ceramic moldings add interest to plain walls. By tiling part of the way up a wall, the designer creates the illusion of wainscoting. Chair rails can be constructed of picture tiles, while entire murals will add visual interest and open up the space.

ON THE WALLS

Tiles have been used to face and ornament walls for hundreds of years. Set into mortar, they become a part of the architecture as well as a part of the design scheme. Because they are semi-permanent elements and not easily removed, it is important to have a well-planned design that you will want to keep for a long time. Drama and excitement can be created by strategic placement of tiles rather than by wild designs that may quickly tire your eyes. The complete arrangement of tiles is just as important (if not more important) as the pattern of any single one.

Wall tiles are traditionally used in baths, powder rooms, and kitchens; however, they are also increasingly being used in sun rooms, exercise rooms, and breakfast nooks. It is by no means necessary to tile a whole room or even a whole wall. Fireplaces can be trimmed or framed in tiles; hallways and corridors can be tiled one-third, one-half, or even two-thirds of the way to the ceiling. A decorative border just under the ceiling will add interest to an otherwise drab hallway.

Although the beauty of ceramic tile is reason enough to use it in any decorating scheme, its durability and practically maintenance-free surface make it particularly suitable for areas where cleanliness might be a problem.

These French mural tiles (left) *create an ornate environment for the serving bar below. A tiled ceiling, as in this bathroom* (right), *is an attractive alternative for bathrooms and kitchens alike.*

Left: A personal or national emblem provides a truly custom look to any tile arrangement. Right: These metallic tiles impart a touch of baronial splendor to this small bath. Far right: These opulent hand-painted Giralda tiles from Spain were derived from Moorish designs that have been used in Spain since 712 A.D.

OVER HEAD AND UNDER FOOT

In the fifteenth century, decorative ceramic tile was used to face ceilings. Set between heavy wooden beams, these brightly colored relief tiles served as insulation and orna-mentation. Today, these same tiles are collector's items, well-preserved and occasionally reset into homes.

Traditionally, however, tiles were most commonly used on floors. Their durability and practicality made them a natural. During the Middle Ages, European countries used brown and yellow encaustic relief tiles. In Renaissance Italy, terra cotta and brightly colored, glazed ceramic tiles were used on the floors. Italian companies still make decorative floor tiles, including contemporary graphic patterns and country florals.

Today there is a strong preference for natural stones, or

© Phillip Ennis; Interior Design by David Hering & John Landau

for glazed floor tiles that resemble stone. Country Floors has pioneered the introduction of rustic tumbled marbles, in all shapes and sizes, as well as cross-cut travertines, treated limestones, and mosaics. The emphasis is on maintaining the hand-hewn, traditional look. The stone look has also been achieved in glazed floor tiles that do not require the maintenance that natural stone does, but can nevertheless be every bit as beautiful.

The most popular of all floor tiles are the unglazed terra cotta tiles available from France, Spain, Peru, and Italy. These tiles come in different sizes and shapes and can be used either by themselves or in combination with other tiles. Square terra cotta tiles from France matched with small glazed tiles is a classic combination. Other shapes— octagons, oblongs, and triangles—can be combined in interesting patterns. Of particular interest is the Italian San Miniato relief tile, an unglazed terra cotta tile with a Romanesque pattern.

Even the simplest installation of terra cotta tiles adds character to an entrance or hallway. The subtle modulations of tone in these terra cotta patios give their respective spaces an enduring, antique look.

© Richard Moreno

The surface of terra cotta varies depending on the method of production and how the terra cotta is altered when it is drying. On some terra cotta tiles, clay is finely sifted and molded to make a smooth surface. On others the clay used is coarse and slightly irregular. Many terra cotta tiles are adorned with some sort of imprint on the surface. There are rustic terra cottas that have the imprints of a dog or a chicken that happened to walk over the tiles as they were drying in the sun. In France, leaves were sometimes pressed into the clay leaving an imprint after the leaf was burned out during the firing.

Octagonal and square terra cottas sometimes contain small glazed tiles called *olambrillas*. These olambrillas vary depending on the country of origin. For example, in France the colored glazed inserts are usually solid colors combined with a large octagon. In Spain and Portugal, the glazed inserts are polychrome or blue decorated tiles with Moorish motifs, shields, or animals. They combine with rectangles to form a basket weave or squares to form a continual off-center square. In Italy, the inserts were *napolitano* or *vietri* designs cut into squares to form an octagonal shape.

Always handsome and long-lasting, terra cotta makes an especially attractive pavement for patios and terraces. Both indoor and outdoor stairways become lovely focal points when paved in terra cotta, especially when paired with glazed decorative tiles. Terra cotta is particularly valued in high stress or heavy traffic areas. In fact, some terra cotta tiles are so strong that they are used to pave driveways. Even more so than wall tiles, floor tiles have become a part of the architecture and serve as a background or canvas for furniture and other decorative elements.

Left: These uniform terra cotta tiles set in a brick design enhance the contemporary look of the staircase. Above: Hexagons produce a more traditional look. Right: The herringbone pattern has a somewhat formal appearance.

AMBIENCE

Tiles are among the most versatile decorating elements available for evoking a wide variety of atmospheres. They are particularly useful for creating a period effect, a regional flavor, and a particular mood or feeling. By carefully choosing between handmade and factory-made tiles, shades of color and types of pattern, size, shape, and angle of tile, you can create an ambience which suits your own personality. A subtle manipulation of the same tools can solve whatever decorating problems you might have.

These Boa Vista rustic wall tiles from Portugal have been hand-molded and hand-painted in a similar manner for over four hundred years. They give an old-world look to any room.

© Ashod Kassabian; Interior Design by Renee Leonard

DRAMATIC IMPACT

A tile design with a dramatic impact is one that will quicken the pulse of everyone who steps into the room. It will surprise them and stop them dead in their tracks. As opposed to a modest tile treatment waiting to catch a passing glance, a dramatic treatment is one that nobody can miss.

FIGURE 4-1

© Richard Moreno

Above: *This mural, whose motif was inspired by an art nouveau design, creates unusual excitement in the bath. Above right: Hand-painted Cocina tiles from Spain lend color and di-* *mension to this kitchen backsplash. Opposite page: These hand-painted oriental figures, which form a sensational backdrop for this serving bar, are works of art in and of themselves.*

Drama is created primarily through commanding position and the use of bold color contrasts; risky, unexpected designs; mysterious shadows; exotic themes; and evocative suggestions. Position is crucial in creating drama. Give the tile area center stage—a space easily seen and uncluttered by furniture. The size and scale of the tile design should be such that it cannot be ignored. Through the use of vivid contrasts, interesting texture variations, and bold color combinations you can create a mysterious, dramatic design that is completely unique.

TILE STYLE

FIGURE 4-2

In Figure 4-1 the design dominates the room. Here, shades of midnight blue and deep lavender were used to create a background of sultry, mysterious, reflected light. This bathroom is sheer fantasy—a gold foil Oriental goddess riding a mythical bird. Seemingly inspired by Aubrey Beardsley, one of England's foremost practitioners of the graceful Art Nouveau style, the mural was hand painted in Italy on machine-made tiles. The sweeping feathers of the goddess' hat curve backward in a wide arc that echoes the shape of the sink.

Black tiles evoke a feeling of mystery and drama. This dusky wet bar (Figure 4-2) is the height of sophisticated drama. The glowing black tiles serve as a background for the delicate brush strokes of the contrasting picture tiles. The high-gloss surface catches the fluttering light and shadows, which are reflected in the sparkle of the cocktail glasses suspended overhead. The meticulously hand-painted oriental figures, imported from Holland, contribute an old-world elegance as well as a highly dramatic and colorful impact.

FIGURE 4-3

While black and dark blue provide the starting points for drama, vibrant colors in unusual mixtures can also elicit strong reactions in a tile project or interior design. In Figure 4-3, shades of deep pink riot with turquoise, green, sky blue, melon, and lavender to produce a bathroom that is eclectic yet unified. The composition is characterized not only by an unusual mix of colors, but by the amalgamation of checkerboard, linear, and geometric patterns, as well as uncommon shapes and sizes, such as mid-size triangles, tiny squares, and elongated rectangles. The depth of the protruding borders and trim, and the glossy texture of the tiles give the design a three-dimensionality and vibrancy that set it apart from other, more subdued designs. This bathroom is a perfect example of pattern, texture, and color working together to present an overall dramatic impression. This particular line of glossy tiles, made in a staggering combination of colors, shapes, and sizes, is completely American in both origin and spirit.

Left: This riotous assortment of color and shape creates a custom look for the adventurous that is stunningly contemporary. Above: Pink becomes exciting when different shades are combined and accented

with the proper pattern.

Right: Blue and white is the most popular color combination. Here the combination of solid color tiles with pattern provides the contrast needed to show each off to its best advantage.

ROMANTIC FLORALS

In the nineteenth century, Europe went through a period called the Romantic Age. This term referred less to the love between people than it did to the love of nature. In England, writer and artist William Morris, one of the members of a group of artists and designers who called themselves the Pre-Raphaelites, and the art critic John Ruskin, led a revolution in aesthetics that was a reaction against the artificiality of the Industrial Age. They believed that while the Age of Science glorified the mind, it destroyed the spirit. Poets like Samuel Coleridge and William Wordsworth found inspiration in the natural beauty of the country landscape and the peasants who worked the earth. The simple country life—living in tune with the seasons—was a counterforce to the crass materialism found in the city. Societies such as Ruskin's Guild of

FIGURE 4-4

TILE STYLE

Here, a small floral design (left) surrounds the charcuterie panel from Portugal.

Small florals mix well with tag tiles, picture tiles, blanks, and border tiles.

St. George, the Century Guild, the Art Worker's Guild, and the Arts and Crafts Society were formed to celebrate hand-made crafts. Handmade objects, it was believed, contained much more of the soul of the worker than did mass-produced factory products.

This view of nature as an important revitalizing force is still very much alive in the twentieth century. It is no acci-dent that our most immediate associations with the words "romantic" and "romance" evoke images of nature. Misty dawns, hazy twilights, fields of flowers, fruit, and foliage were favorite themes of the nineteenth and twentieth cen-tury artists and designers. Floral patterns, small, delicate, sometimes fussy, and even Victorian in flavor, have emerged as among the most popular in tile design.

As with other types of tiles, the most popular color for floral tiles is blue, but other favorite floral colors include red, yellow, pink, and gold. Small, blue florals can be used to add just the right amount of color to your design scheme to make it pretty but not overpowering. Versatile too, they can be highly decorative, clean and crisp, and even some-what elegant.

The tile mural above the stove in this kitchen (Figure 4-4) has a certain elegant air. The blue cross-hatch floral design around the mural and behind the counter contains touches of yellow and green that add just a hint of color. The raised border tiles above the cabinets and wooden beam are more colorful and elaborate than the blue florals; however, because the pattern is small, interspersed with blank squares, and echoes the cross-hatch pattern of the blue florals, the effect is one of unity.

FIGURE 4-5

Left: What can be more romantic than flowers and a fireplace? Right: This floral mural framed by a small print border gives the illusion of a painting reflected in a mirror.

TILE STYLE

Few things are as romantic as a fireplace, and this one (Figure 4-5), framed by red roses on crisp white tiles, is light, cheery, and romantic. The blue pastel wall and white carved mantle and moldings provide the perfect place for these delicate floral tiles. If placed on a busier backdrop these tiles would be much less prominent; however, on this understated fireplace, they provide a dominant visual focus, demanding attention.

A bouquet of flowers can be just as romantic as an entire meadow. The bathroom in Figure 4-6 uses an arrangement of flowers as the focal point behind the sink. The small floral border and molding tiles echo the larger, more elaborate floral mural. Again here, the white tile provides the perfect background for the vibrancy of the colorful, hand-painted tiles, while creating an open, airy look of delicacy and freshness.

FIGURE 4-6

FIGURE 4-7

Quite different in feel is the tiled bathroom in Figures 4-7 and 4-8. Here, a cross-hatch design similar to that in the kitchen in Figure 4-4 is used; however, the difference in color—pink as opposed to blue—changes the effect completely. The florals in this bathroom take a backseat to the strong use of pattern. The solid-colored pink tiles around the bath are arranged in a diamond shape that complements the patterned tiles above it.

In addition to conveying a feeling of romance, florals impart their own sense of period and place. Boa Vista rustic wall tiles from Portugal have a baroque, baronial flavor; while smaller, delicate Miradouro tiles are more country and contemporary in feeling, and the soft pastels

FIGURE 4-8

of the Valentine hand-painted tiles have a distinct early American quality. The Pastorale tiles from France have a rococo delicacy and flair. Match them with the Provençal terra cotta floor tiles or the Mistral floor tiles in praline and brown. Or create a flower-filled sun room with floral walls and floor tiles from Italy.

Left: This pastel comes to life when it is mixed with pattern. Above and left: These "pastorale" wall tiles from France are delicately hand-painted with seventeenth and eighteenth century motifs that lend a timeless elegance to this contemporary bath.

TRADITIONAL DESIGNS

Many of the designs produced today in factories in Holland, Spain, Italy, and Portugal are the same patterns painted by the factories where they were originated centuries ago. In some cases, such as the Giralda relief tiles from Spain, modern techniques enable the artisans to create tiles that imitate the ancient mosaics. But few tiles are imitations. Rather, they are duplications or continuations of the original designs. Arabesques, geometrics, stylized flora and fauna, heraldic devices, garlands, and lattice designs are all ancient patterns that are still created throughout Europe.

Individual picture tiles, such as delft blue-and-white seascapes and landscapes, peasants working or walking in the field, children playing, animals, birds, and fish, are still being made. Today, tile murals are becoming as popular in contemporary tile design as they were in Renaissance Europe.

Many of these traditional patterns and designs were used to adorn the homes of wealthy aristocrats. They paved their grand interior courtyards and decorated their magnificent fountains. They faced the walls of grand cathedrals and palatial dining rooms.

Depending on how these tiles are arranged, they convey the same sense of splendor and importance as they did in their original setting. Terra cotta tiles, in particular, when mixed with glazed tiles, convey an impressive sense of history and nobility.

These tiles, which have for so long been used as architectural elements, seem at home with other natural building materials such as stone, slate, marble, or wood. While they themselves are rigid, they fit easily into flowing, irregular forms. Greek columns, Moorish arches, and colonial fan windows are all complemented by ceramic tile.

Murals are particularly effective in creating a sense of tradition. A garden wall, an enormous urn overflowing with flowers, and a series of bird cages flanked by flying birds recall the delightful, light-hearted feeling of a lost age. A seascape on a dining room wall or fruits and vegetables in the kitchen convey a sense of nineteenth-century richness.

© Phillip Ennis

This basket of flowers (left) brings a splash of color to this dark corner of the kitchen. These panels of vegetables (right) require only a small space to provide instant visual satisfaction.

TILE STYLE

SLEEK AND MODERN

If one associates nature and the emotions with romanticism, the idea of the modern suggests its polar opposite: industrialism and science. The mind is once again admired, and the product of its knowledge—the machine—has almost become an icon of worship.

In contrast to the designs associated with the Victorian period, modern design emphasizes simplicity and geometry. In the machine age, crisp, clean lines were valued. Architects like Le Corbusier, the pseudonym of Charles-Edouard Jeanneret-Gris (1887-1965), emphasized the importance of open interior space and the free circulation of light and air. The Bauhaus, the famous design school founded in 1919 in Germany, emphasized classic lines and shapes—the uncluttered look. Design was streamlined and simplified. Form followed function.

In modern design, stripes, grids, and abstract shapes replace the flowers and fruits of nature. White is more important than ever before, because of its crispness and its ability to convey the essence of hi-tech style. For the modern look, neutrals such as sand, gray, and every shade of off-white are extremely important. In fact, single-color tiles arranged in a simple checkerboard or striped pattern, convey the contemporary no-nonsense feeling.

Above: *Contemporary art tiles adorn the walls of this modern bathroom. Right: A beautiful fireplace with playful grid work.*

Opposite page: *Tiles with a neutral color scheme come alive with the right accent. Note that the chevron matches the border.*

DECORATING WITH TILES

In its celebration of the machine, the scientific, and the mathematical, the modern style seems particularly suited to the city with its high-rise apartments and avant-garde architecture. To create this feeling, choose primarily factory-made tiles, whose uniformity of thickness and shape emphasizes crisp lines. Machine-glazed tiles help provide the sleek, even look desired in modern design. Less pattern rather than more will also enhance the overall contemporary effect. Another option is to use asymmetrically spaced combinations of plain and patterned tiles.

Metallics can also be quite effective in creating a contemporary ambience—either used alone or mixed with matte

tiles. When set on an angle, tiles establish a geometric pattern, creating their own visual interest. Although a sleek, modern look can be easily attained, tiles are such a traditional building material that even when they are most modern in spirit, they create a sense of the past, bringing some warmth into even the most hi-tech surroundings.

Far left: Glazed black tiles are a dramatic backdrop for a display of treasured objects. Center: The edges of the black tiles form a grid which introduces pattern into the space. Above: This chevron design with its metallic border brings a contemporary touch to the traditional architecture. Below: This narrow border framing the arch infuses a Mediterranean flavor.

This modern bathroom (Figure 4-9), with its metallic and white chevron tiles, is reminiscent of tin ceilings, gold-leaf mosaics, and old brass buttons. The chevron pattern in the shower provides a contrast to the gold-leaf tiles and moldings and the plain wallpaper. The same tiles are used successfully in hallway and outdoor designs.

The simple blue tile combined with the white lattice in this bathroom(Figure 4-10)shows the popularity of grids in modern design. In this installation, the blue tile is used sparingly, its large solid blocks contrasting the checked effect of the grid. The same design is used much more liberally around the bath in Figure 4-11. Here the blue tile gives a marbled effect, broken only by the white molding running around the circumference of the room.

FIGURE 4-9

FIGURE 4-10

FIGURE 4-11

Left: *Variation in color in these terra cotta tiles enhances the traditional flavor of this kitchen.* Opposite page, left: *Mix these glorious Culinarios kitchen wall tiles from Portugal to create murals of hanging produce, mouth-watering fruits and vegetables, and assorted species of fresh fish.* Opposite page, right: *This rustic Italian Maiolica was hand-painted in the styles of the seventeenth and eighteenth centuries.*

RUSTIC

History seems to be a series of repeating patterns, like tiles themselves. If the eighteenth century was named the Age of Reason for its belief in science, and the nineteenth century was called the Age of Romanticism because it celebrated the spirit and emotions, the twentieth century has experienced a series of movements.

In America, the Arts and Crafts Movement, which lasted from 1879 through the 1920s, was a reaction against the Industrial Age. It was soon followed by a counter reaction that resulted in the modern style, a celebration of the Industrial Age, which extended into the 1960s. Then, once again, there was a reversal. Since the 1960s, Americans—

and to some extent Europeans, particularly the English— have turned away from the city back to the country for inspiration in lifestyle and design. Once more the beauty of nature is celebrated as the salve to the starving spirit. Friendly, comfortable, easy—these designs are not intended to jar the sensibilities or make bold dramatic statements.

Tile design reflects this movement in its adaptation of floral prints, birds, and animal designs. Colors are toned down for a more intimate feeling, while busier bursts of pattern or repeated patterns are accepted. Solid-colored tiles are especially valued too, particularly those that are handmade and hand-painted and can convey a personal expression.

Handmade and hand-glazed tiles convey the rustic look

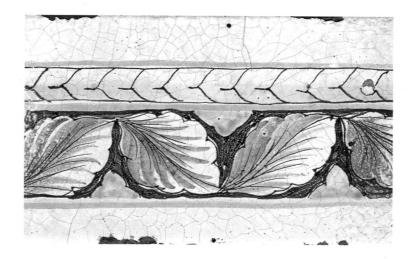

most effectively. Mexican tiles on the walls, with their freely drawn pictures of flowers, birds, and fruits, combined with unglazed terra cotta on the floor evokes a comfortable, unpretentious look.

The best murals for this kind of ambience are the Culinarios panels of hanging game and vegetables from Portugal. Also, blue and white tag tiles impart a marvelous provincial flavor, striking a balance between pattern and plain. The combination can be either regular or random, a repeated, expected rhythm of pattern and plain, or a casual, sudden burst of pattern. Concentrate on a few colors, either pale or intense. To make the most of texture, use matte-glazed tiles rather than high-gloss glazes. Mixing textures and patterns will add to the casual, relaxed atmosphere of any room.

FIGURE 4-12

Below: A traditional border combined with a terra cotta floor brings a country flavor into this kitchen. Right: The distribution of patterned and plain tiles leads the eye upward expanding the sense of space in the room.

THE COUNTRY FLOORS LOOK

The Country Floors look, whether it is in a private house, a patio, a hotel, or a restaurant, combines patterned wall tiles and rustic terra cotta or stone floors knit together with four-hundred years of tile heritage. It is a look that is European and traditional, but is presented with such flair and boldness that it is at home in a contemporary setting.

Many visitors to Portugal, Spain, France, and Italy are awestruck by the grandeur of ancient tile installations. They marvel at the Alcazar in Seville, a small restaurant in Naples, a cheese shop in Paris, or a storefront in Lisbon. Each of these installations represents the tradition of centuries of tile handiwork. They have been altered and revised through years of repairs, changes, additions, and wear, resulting in an unusual amalgamation of differing patterns, panels, and borders.

The twenty-five-year-old installation in Figure 4-12, called Portuguese Paella, starts with one Portuguese pattern on one side of the room, but switches along the

way to another totally different Portuguese pattern and border. The stove hood is made of Spanish tiles from Seville, the walls are from Portuguese panels, and the floor is from Italy. The designer even went to the extent of using broken tiles and intentionally breaking tiles and mismatching sizes in order to imitate the look of ancient European tile installations.

Another aspect of this look is achieved through the liberal use of panel tiles, blanks with corner designs, and border tiles. By installing panels over rows of patterned borders a wainscot effect can be achieved. Another effective use of panels is to install them from the floor to the ceiling with borders going around the doors and windows of the room. Panels of fish hanging on a row of hooks, pheasants and rabbits, and garlic, onions, and carrots can be installed in a row high in the room to appear as one long rack of food waiting to be cooked.

The liberal use of decorative borders, panels, and the juxtapositioning of patterns and elements are key to the Country Floors look.

While the end effect of the Country Floors look constitutes many elements juxtaposed in a seemingly spontaneous way, these installations require careful planning and a special attention to detail. They may be austerely simple, or abundantly ornate; they are never boring.

ACCENTS &ACCESSORIES

While the tile treatment of any room will transform it into the realm of the unusual, accents and accessories can add that special touch that makes it feel like home.

Since Norman Karlson, owner/founder of Country Floors, started his career as a photographer, he always had an eye for props. It was only natural for him to adorn his tile showroom with the kinds of accessories that had been so useful in his photographs—a vase of flowers, a beautiful ceramic dish, a terra cotta planter, a hand-painted platter. The same decorating touches that personalized his photos now transform his formal showroom into an intimate space.

Many of the same factories that produce tile also create platters, planters, and vases—after all, they too are ceramic and require similar artisan skills as well as the same kilns and clay. Many people want to buy the soap dish that matches the tiles of their sink. They want to take home the same vase of flowers they had admired on the tiled kitchen counter.

One of Country Floors' most exciting discoveries was a factory near Florence that specializes in producing apothecary jars. For centuries these covered jars—elaborately hand-painted with traditional floral designs in blue, orange, and green—had been used to hold medicinal herbs and powders. Even today many pharmacists in Italy still proudly display these brightly colored jars as a symbol of their profession.

Part of the charm of the jars, in ancient times as well as today, was the Latin—or more precisely pseudo-Latin—lettering which was an integral part of the design. The fine calligraphy was an admired art in itself, but Latin—the language of the educated and the religious class—elevated the design and endowed the apothecary jar with almost magical properties.

Today, language scholars have shown that many of the words were made up by the artisans, whose background in Latin was limited. Other words have no translation in modern terms because the strange herbs and mixtures they identified have been lost in time. Still other words, like *Fructus* (fruit), are still recognizable today. The use of calligraphy also appealed to tile designers.

The psuedo-Latin lettering on these apothecary jars and vases appealed to a large number of tile designers who borrowed from these styles.

The Lion and the Foo Dog (right) are examples of Italian ceramic artistry.

The designs of these museum replica apothecary jars and figure bottles (above and right) *show their close relationship to tile design.*

In addition, many Italian factories produce complete lines of fifteenth and sixteenth century museum reproductions. Beakers, pitchers, bottles, and carafes, authentic in every respect down to the misspelled Latin wording, are finding their way into many houses and apartments.

Several factories have been producing traditional ceramic wares for centuries. Heraldic designs—griffins, lions, dragons—have always been extremely popular, each noble family having its own distinctive coat of arms. Reaching back into their archives, these factories resur- rected ancient designs and began to produce pitchers, vases and jars for a new audience. Plaques featuring these designs and the closely related state emblems could be fastened onto a stucco wall or embedded in a wall faced with decorative tile.

A factory in Spain now produces emblems of many European countries—and even America. Made up of twelve tiles, these plaques are mini-murals. These emblems and plaques seem to have a special attraction. Families can now have their own coat of arms or proudly display the emblem of the European nation where their ancestors were born.

These personalized, identifying plaques were related to another kind of ceramic plaque long used in Europe; plaques that carried the street name fastened to corner

buildings. Individual buildings and private residences often carried a plaque with the street number and even the name of the family living within.

These plaques are now custom produced by a factory in Portugal. Individual tiles with the proper letters and numbers can be combined, surrounded by a floral border or leafy trim, and made into a small mural. Or, the name itself, handwritten, can be produced on a single tile, custom-ordered from the factory.

As one thing leads to another, tile makers immediately took to the notion of letters on ceramic tiles. Some were then incorporated into children's rooms—why not alphabet tiles instead of alphabet blocks? These have developed from the traditional "tag tiles" used in many countries of Europe to identify wines, herbs, and other foodstuffs in store rooms and cellars.

Still produced in Portugal, these charming blue and white tiles identify and label twenty-four kinds of wine, including Beaujolais, Bordeaux, Bourgogne, Chablis, Margaux, Nuits St. Georges, Pommard, and Riesling, to mention a few.

Emblems and tag tiles are popular accents to well-planned tile installations.

One factory has been making these Giardino terra cotta planters (left) since 1660. Each piece bears the authentic seal registered by the Italian crown. This tile-topped chest (right) makes a great poolside table.

ACCENTS & ACCESSORIES

Herbs and foodstuffs, such as onions, oil and vinegar, and pepper—or more precisely "oignons," "huile et vinaigre," and "poivre" since all the tags are in French—are now available. There are 120 possibilities in all. The tile tags were originally also made in English but the French aura in wine and food won out. C'est la vie.

While the hand-painted jars and plaques are joyfully colorful, there is another group of accessories more subdued but equally exciting. Like the terra cotta tiles that have been adorning the floors of manor houses, villas, and churches for hundreds of years, terra cotta pots from the rich clay of Tuscany have been produced since the fifteenth century. The rich, red patina of these pots, hand-finished to emphasize the edges of the decorative relief,

provide a warmth that only natural clay can impart. Decorated with a frieze of cupids, fruits, seashells, and acanthus leaves, these terra cotta planters evoke architectural images of the ancient Roman empire. Pedestals, urns, pots, and even stools are produced from this Italian factory, giving any residence a baronial air. In particular, these

unglazed accessories complement the polished surface of a painted tile wall or provide a three-dimensional accent to a terra cotta patio.

Ceramic furniture comes next, a natural progression to lovers of ceramic tile. For years, do-it-yourselfers bought tiles and set them into table tops for beautiful dining tables, patio tables, and cocktail tables. There are even hand-painted, ceramic tabletops, imported from Italy, with decorative wrought iron bases. The table top features a traditional design in blue, orange, yellow, and green, a tangle of gorgeous foliage and exotic florals.

Country Floors has a line of hand-painted sinks that is unique in the field. Crossing the line between accent, accessory, and furniture, these distinctive works of art are produced in France in three traditional styles: the wall basin, the corner basin, and the wall lavabo. Featuring a delicate design of birds, flowers, and shells, in gold, blue, and brown, they lend an aura of elegance to any bath- or powder-room. A matching mirror and soap dish is also available. These sinks can be used within a total bath treatment of decorative ceramic tile or form the focal point of a treatment made up primarily of monotonal tiles.

While these three styles are available, other designs and patterns can be custom-painted to match the surrounding tile, wallpaper, or fabric in the room.

Among the most beautiful ceramic accessories, and probably the ones most closely related to tiles, are hand-painted platters and plates. Six- and ten-inch animal, geometrical, and botanical plates are imported from Italy.

Oval and octagon landscape platters, round fish platters, square florals, even ceramic soup ladles come from Portugal. A group of bold primitive plates, from Spain, as well as a series of authentic reproductions of garlands, flowers, fruits, and geometricals are from the seventeenth century. All the Spanish plates make lovely wall decorations. Don't look for sets of serving dishes here—each one is different and there are no cups, saucers, or bowls. Tables can be set with some of the serving platters from Portugal and in particular the "Primula" pattern, a charming, provincial red and green floral print on a glossy white background. Complete sets are available. Candlesticks and soup tureens from Portugal complete a table suitable for your most honored guests.

Ceramic accents and accessories set off the tile treatment of any room or add interest to other home furnishings. The glow and color of these natural materials add a treasured warmth and tradition in an age where so much is artificial and transitory.

The delicate design of this hand-painted sink (opposite page) will add floral elegance to any bathroom. Folclore platters from Spain (left) and Fianca platters from Portugal (above) show the variety of hand-painted ceramic accessories.

COLLECTING ANTIQUE TILES

The Portuguese have been making tiles in the same manner for over four hundred years. This antique picture tile (above) was carefully molded and painted by hand, as were the more recently made Obidos tiles surrounding the fireplace.

For those who love color, pictorial design, and bold graphics, the beauty of tiles is excuse enough for collecting them. But even beyond the purely visual interest, is the sense of history captured in tile art. From the heraldic designs of the fourteenth century, through the Renaissance representations of Greek gods, to the eighteenth century pictures of Dutch seascapes, to the nineteenth century of portraiture, Chinese landscapes, and Art Nouveau florals, to the twentieth century of Art Deco foliage and contemporary geometrics, tile art encapsulates not only the history of design, but major social and economic movements throughout Europe and the United States.

English medieval tiles, for example, often have an eastern flavor, since tile art was already established in the Middle East and slowly moved west as a result of trade and conquering armies. The earthquake in 1755 that destroyed half of Lisbon resulted in an enormous expansion in the manufacture of tiles crucial to rebuilding the city. In Europe, the increased trade with China and Japan in the nineteenth century is reflected in the Chinese themes incorporated into the English tiles of that period. In America, the Arts and Crafts Movement (1870–1920) that stimulated interest in handmade objects eventually gave rise to a whole new tile-making industry embracing native themes.

Picture tiles are particularly evocative of the past, capturing scenes from contemporary life as if in a photograph or painting. Nineteenth

century English tiles show games, portraits of famous actors, and scenes from well-known novels. Sixteenth-century relief tiles from Spain and nineteenth-century floral floor tiles from Italy bring the splendor of a bygone era to life once again.

AGE AND ACCESSIBILITY

Spanish tiles are the oldest tiles in Europe and there are many available for collectors that date from 1350 to 1450. Portuguese tiles from before the earthquake of 1755 are rare. After that date, however, the industry expanded so enormously that tiles are relatively plentiful. Those made in the period directly after the earthquake are known as Pombalinos, after Pombol, the chamberlain who took charge of rebuilding Lisbon. These blue-and-white tiles, depicting classical themes or well-dressed men and women, often occur in sets of several tiles which together form a mural. A collector can often get a bargain on a "fragment" (one tile) of such a set.

For the collector of English tiles, the most prolific period was from 1850 to 1910. During this period a number of technical advances allowed for a general expansion of the industry. Victorian and Edwardian tiles show the stylistic influence of naturalism, classicism, neo-Gothic revivalism, Oriental motifs, the Arts and Crafts Movement, and Art Nouveau.

Constable encouraged observation in painting and nature became a favorite tile theme. Classicism was also popular during this period, and Grecian vases, garlands of fruit and flowers, acanthus leaves and olive branches, winged cherubs, and lions are often found. The architect Pugin favored the medieval encaustic tiles and encouraged their reproduction. The most popular neo-Gothic elements were the fleur-de-lis and the revival of the four-tile pattern.

The hand-painted tiles of well-dressed men and women (above) *were used as part of the rebuilding of Lisbon after the earthquake of 1755.*

These Pastorale stanniferous wall tiles (left) *from France use seventeenth and eighteenth century motifs from Flanders to create an elaborate floral touch to this modern bathroom.*

The Chinese influence is found in exotic birds and landscapes. Bold, simple designs inspired by wood-block prints found their way to England from Japan. Especially valued were blossoming branches and chrysanthemums, the latter a symbol of imperial Japan.

William De Morgan is a name to remember as one of the most important designers of the Arts and Crafts Movement in England. He adapted the simple but bold lines and forms from the Persians and Japanese. Morgan's lithographic printing technique was especially suited to reproduce flat areas of color.

Art Nouveau design flourished at the end of the nineteenth century and the beginning of the twentieth. Its main characteristic was its flowing, sensuous lines. Relief patterns that simulated the technique of tube-lining were particularly successful in emphasizing the beauty of the

The Chinese influence can be seen in the exotic birds and trees of these mural tiles (opposite page). Thick, marble-textured and plain glazes, were popular during the 1920s and 30s.

meandering line.

During the 1920s and 30s, abstract art began to influence English tile design, and many pictures were replaced by geometrics. Marble-textured glazes, used to frame fireplaces, and plain glazes gained favor.

Although more scarce than the other tiles, medieval floor tiles can also be found. Usually of red clay with a white decoration, covered with a lead glaze before firing, the resulting tile was brown and yellow. Although some of these tiles date from the beginning of the thirteenth century, their prices are often no higher than those of nineteenth century tiles since many collectors find their muted colors even less appealing after centuries of wear. Nevertheless, since the style and technique of medieval tiles were revived during the Victorian period, the collector can find historical interest in these early tiles.

Dutch tiles from the 1700s on can be found. Delft tiles have been collector's items for many years and are well represented in antique stores throughout Europe and the United States. The Dutch tile industry centered first in Rotterdam and then spread to Haarlem, Delft, Gouda, Utrecht, and later to Friesland.

The factory in Makkum is still making tiles today and has been owned by the same family since the seventeenth century. As a gift to Norman Karlson when he opened his New York store, the president of the Makkum factory gave him a portrait of the Stadholder (Governor) of the Province of Friesland, made during his lifetime, somewhere between 1711 and 1751. Made of six tiles, it shows a stately figure mounted on a rearing horse.

Because the Dutch traded with the Far East, Chinese porcelain had a distinct influence on Dutch tiles, not only in the blue and white colors, but also thematically. In the second half of the seventeenth century, however, Dutch painting and engraving began to have an effect on the tile industry, and subject matter from the immediate environment began to be pictured. A peculiar characteristic of the Dutch tile is a pin hole at each corner made by nails that secured the tiles to a board during the cutting process.

Delft tiles are traditional collector's items and can be found in antique stores throughout Europe. The traditional Dutch wall tiles on these two pages were all produced by the same factory in Makkum. This family-owned business has been making tiles since the seventeenth century.

The tile details (left) depict traditional themes found on Dutch tiles. Top and bottom are Dutch landscapes. The figures on the center tiles are examples of the Chinese influence caused by Dutch trade with the Far East.

The delicate tulip pattern (left) is a reproduction of a turn-of-the-century English transfer tile.

In the eighteenth century, English Delftware began to compete with the Dutch for the market. Generally, the Dutch tiles are whiter than the English, which have a bluish tinge. One distinguishing feature of the English Delftware made in Bristol is a white-on-white border ornament (bianco-sopra-bianco).

In the United States, the most collectible tiles are those from the Arts and Crafts Movement (1870–1920). Among the most well-known factories was the one on Catalina Island, owned by the Wrigley Gum family. The two largest American tile factories of that period were the American Encaustic Tile Company and the Mosaic Tile Co., both in

© Phillip Ennis

It is difficult to find antique Italian tiles, since most were used on floors and subsequently demolished or worn. These present-day Italian tiles use soft patterns to compliment current environments.

Zanesville, Ohio. But factories flourished in Massachusetts, New York, New Jersey, Colorado, California, Michigan, and Pennsylvania, rivaling in quantity the tile output of any country in Europe.

It is difficult to find antique Italian, French, or German tiles today. Most of the decorated Italian tiles were used for floors, so they were either demolished when the building was demolished or worn by use.

Ancient tiles from the Middle East (Iran, Israel, and Egypt) can be found, but the buyer must beware. Many so-called ancient tiles are produced for the tourist trade.

PRICE

Tiles are still relatively inexpensive, and, strangely enough, age is not usually the determining factor. Most single, ancient Spanish tiles from the 1400s, Portuguese tiles from the late 1700s, English tiles from the late 1800s and American tiles from the late 1900s, all cost approximately the same—about $200–250. Sets, like the Midsummer Night's Dream (Wedgwood, late 1800s) that contained several tiles, cost considerably more. Series, like the Days of the Week (Minton's China Works, 1880s) and Aesop's Fables (Minton Hollins, 1875) are in demand by collectors and cost more.

Like any of the arts, certain famous names, makers with a wide reputation, command higher prices. Well-known English tile makers include The Minton Tile Companies, Campbell Brick and Tile Co., W.T. Copeland & Sons, Maw & Company, Josiah Wedgwood & Sons, Pilkington's Tile & Pottery Co., and William De Morgan—firms that flourished in the late nineteenth and early twentieth centuries.

In the United States, the most well-known tile makers were The Low Art Tile Company (Chelsea, Mass.), Bennington Pottery (Bennington, Vt.), The American Encaus-

This floral mural (left) was made at Royal Makkum, in Holland, one of the oldest and most famous Dutch factories. The Moorish influence can be seen in these Giralda relief tiles from Spain. Cuisiniere wall tiles from Spain (right) are successfully combined with Portuguese panels.

DECORATING WITH TILES

tic Tiles Co. (Zanesville, Ohio), The Trent Tile Company (Trenton, New Jersey), The Star Encaustic Company (Pittsburgh, Pa.), and Rookwood Pottery (Cincinnati, Ohio), whose height of production was from 1875–1920.

The American Encaustic Tiles Co. was well-known for its relief tiles designed by Herman Mueller, a German immigrant. The Trent Tile Company produced a unique matte-finished tile, made by sand blasting the relief after glazing. Designer William Wood Gallimore later gained a reputation as a prolific artist and sculptor.

The Rookwood Pottery owed its fame to Mrs. Maria Longworth Nicols, whose family supported the experimental enterprise for nine years until it became financially independent. Most of the artists employed came

For an antique look at a modest price, these white relief tiles from Mexico are a nice alternative.

from local art schools in Cincinnati. One exception was Kataro Shirayamadani, a Japanese artist whose work was notable for its Oriental motifs.

Another notable woman in the American tile arena was Miss Louise McLaughlin, founder of the Pottery Club and Associated Artists of Cincinnati. An expert pottery and tile decorator, she encouraged other women to learn these arts.

DATING

Dating tiles is a tricky process and forgeries do exist. Color and theme will give collectors some clue. Methods of printing or transferring design also provide some information. Thickness can be used to some extent as a guide, with the older tiles usually being thicker than the more modern ones. But the most "scientific" method of dating tiles is by the maker's marks, stamps and designs on the back of the tile. Each manufacturer imprinted the back of his tiles with a distinctive design and/or stamp at various times that are recorded in books accessible to tile collectors.

Registration numbers may also appear in the form of a diamond-shaped mark containing letters and numbers. These marks were used between 1842 and 1883 in England. After 1883, the letters "R.d" (registered) appeared, followed by a series of consecutive numbers. These numbers and marks were issued by the Patent Office in London in an attempt to protect original designs and are recorded in the Public Records office at Kew in London.

At left is a genuine eighteenth-century Portuguese panel made for the restoration of Lisbon after the earthquake of 1755. The other tile designs featured here are modern replicas or contemporary versions of antique designs.

Portuguese Miradouro wall tiles (left) are modern versions of ancient designs.

CONDITION

Condition will affect price just as it would a vase or piece of antique furniture. If the piece is rare enough, a chip or even a crack will not seriously detract from the price. Nevertheless, a tile in good or perfect condition will usually cost more. Once upon a time repairs used to be made with metal clips. Nowadays, restorers can touch up paint, even reglaze sections of a tile, and glue pieces together so the appearance is not seriously marred. Bear in mind, however, that such skilled repair work is expensive, costing a minimum of $150.00. Since the buyer must add the cost of a repair on to the cost of the tile, and yet lower the price of the tile upon resale because it has been repaired, expensive repairs are often not worth doing.

Old tiles may need cleaning. Small scratches in the glaze can be made less visible with household soap. The back of the tiles can be cleaned the same way or rubbed with steel wool. Do not use steel wool on the glazed surface, however. Paint on the glazed surface can be cleaned with paint stripper. After cleaning, allow the tile to dry and then rub with a dry cloth to restore the luster. Cement clinging to the back of the tile can present a problem. Often it can be scraped away with a knife, or soaked in water until it loosens.

While many tiles can still be found for $10.00 or $20.00, some tiles can be quite expensive—and the prices are going up. Mr. Karlson recently bought 980 fourteenth century tiles and the wood beams that housed them, which were used to face the underside of a roof in Seville. Although these tiles are almost 400 years old, their vivid colors and relief design show little sign of wear. Since they were on the inside of the roof, they were exposed neither to the elements nor the sole of man. Originally purchased by William Randolph Hearst, they were sold at auction in the 1950s and set into a house in Santa Rosa. Five years ago, a pair of tiles in a similar design from the same period were selling in Spain for $25.00. Today the same two tiles are selling for $427.00.

© Phillip Ennis; Interior Design by Susan Kelly

Picture tiles provide a visual treat, whether around a fireplace (left) or in a kitchen (right). Note the fine use of ceramic tiles interspersed on the terra cotta floor in the kitchen.

MARKETS

Most tiles can be purchased from antique dealers. European tile is easily found throughout Western Europe, and English tile is particularly well represented in antique shops throughout England.

In the United States, the dealers most likely to carry antique tiles are those who handle deco and nouveau pottery. Occasionally tiles do come up at auction and several years ago Sotheby's auctioned off a collection of fireplace tiles from Holland and Germany.

There are several large fairs where antique tiles can be found. In the United States, the best place for American tile is the July exhibition in Zanesville, Ohio, called The Pottery Lovers' Reunion. Since several of the largest American tile companies were located in or around Zanesville, tiles here have long been valued and collected. Another important showplace for collectors is the pottery exhibition held in October in Los Angeles, and the April antique fair in New York City.

DISPLAY

Some antique tiles are so lovely they can stand alone, like a work of art. Collectors can purchase a wire mounting and hang them, like a painting or a plate, on the wall. Several tiles can be combined and mounted together in a frame. The most attractive mountings, however, expose the edges of the tile. Slanted shelves are ideal for showing off an extensive collection, but small groupings of tile can be set up on top of a mantel, leaning against a book shelf, resting on a tabletop.

Antique tiles can also be permanently reset in a wall, a fireplace, or any area where they would serve as an accent. It is often possible to buy sets of twenty or more tiles from antique dealers which are usually enough to frame a fireplace. Country Floors has several patterns of old Portuguese tiles available for sale. Resetting antique tiles is one way to bring a little bit of history into the contemporary scene.

Because tiles are so long lasting, the tiles you buy today will be tomorrow's valuable collectible. Bringing with them beauty, durability, and history, ceramic tiles are unique building blocks that link the past with the future.

© Julius Shulman; Interior Design by Lillian Chain, A.S.I.D.

MEASUREMENT, MATHEMATICS & MAINTENANCE

■ ■ ■ ■ ■ ■ ■ ■ ■ ■ ■

There comes a time in every decorating project where the armchair fantasies finally have to give way to practical considerations. You know what look or feeling you want. You even know how to create that look or feeling. Before making your final choice, you have to be sure that the tiles you choose are suitable for that particular area. If they are for a patio or pool and the temperature in your area is likely to go below freezing, you have to be sure that your tiles are frost resistant. If you are thinking of using the tiles for a kitchen counter or bar, be sure you choose tiles that are acid resistant. Be sure you select the correct type of tiles for the walls and floors.

Think about the amount of wear and use the area is going to receive and choose tiles accordingly.

Very Light Stress: Suitable for light use: kitchen, bath and wine cellar walls.

Light Stress: Suitable for residential bedroom and powder room floors, or light traffic areas not subject to abrasive eroding materials.

Moderate Stress: Floor tiles suitable for light traffic, residential use such as bathrooms, or areas subject to minimal abrasive eroding materials. Many of the tiles in this category may also be used on residential kitchen and dining room floors. However, bear in mind that they are not totally wear or impact resistant. These tiles can also be used as a

decorative inset with floor tile suited to heavy stress.
Normal Stress: Suitable for residential kitchen and hallway floors; also light traffic commercial floors such as
reception areas, offices and boutiques, or any areas
subject to normal foot traffic and abrasive materials.

Heavy stress: Suitable for commercial floors, patios, terraces, and balconies with minimal exposure to moisture.
    After you've satisfied the stress and wear requirements,
the next problem to tackle is how many and how much.
How many tiles are needed to face that fireplace? How
many to finish that kitchen floor? And, of course, how
much will it all cost? Cost is related to the number of tiles
which is related to the size of tiles. All three have to
somehow be mixed together to come out with something
you can afford.

Terra cotta tiles are available in a variety of shapes and sizes. Made to handle varying stress, terra cotta has been used on floors, patios, even driveways.

There are too many ways of setting and sealing tiles to discuss here. Each type of tile and surface has its own demands. Nevertheless, there are some guidelines to bear in mind.

In many houses that have settled, the floors and walls will not exactly line up. Therefore, it is often recommended that different size tile be used on the walls and the floors. Tiles will line up best on the straightest walls.

There are many methods of setting and sealing tiles. Choose the one that will best suit the requirements of your installation.

© Jennifer Levy

Tile artisans (right) work diligently at hand-painting tiles. The installation at left is a wonderful example of beautiful hand-painted tiles.

Handmade or hand-painted tiles will have variations in color and shape that can enhance the appearance of the area if installed with an eye to making the most of these variations. Therefore, it is strongly recommended that a craftsperson, who is experienced with handmade tiles, carefully blend the tiles during the installation process. Grout colors should be chosen in most circumstances to blend with the color of the tile. Avoid grout colors which strongly contrast with the color—such as black grout and white tile—as grout color can permanently stain the tile. If it isn't deliberately and carefully planned as a design element, it can be very distracting, competing with the tile itself. Experiment with grout and tile combinations prior to installation. Always buy extra tiles. Cutting tiles can be a tricky process even for the most experienced cutter.

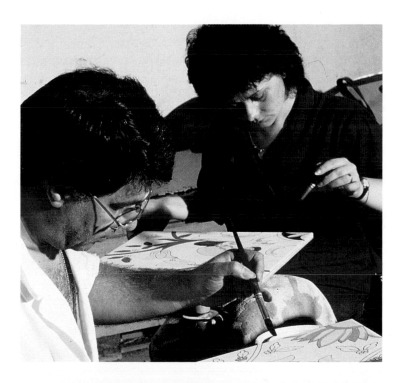

DECORATING WITH TILES

Metallic moldings and luster finishes must be carefully installed so that the finish is not damaged. Special grouting material should be used.

Glazed ceramic tiles are often maintenance free and can be cleaned with a simple detergent or soap and water. Avoid abrasive or acid-based cleaning products on any glazed tile. Metallic glazed tiles contain real metal and should be cleaned with metal polishes.

Terra cotta tile, far and away the most popular flooring, comes from several different countries. Generally, terra cotta is sold untreated and must be properly sealed and maintained to ensure a lifetime of beauty.

Glazed ceramic tiles are virtually maintenance free. Avoid using abrasives or acid-based cleaning products that may damage the surface of the tiles.

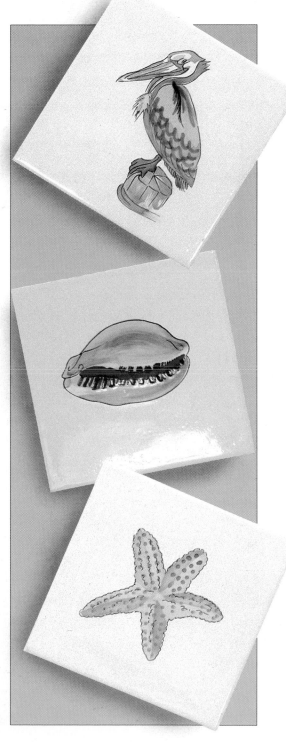

Periodic waxing will enhance the lustre and tone of some terra cotta tiles. Do not wax, however, if the tiles were sealed with polyurethane.

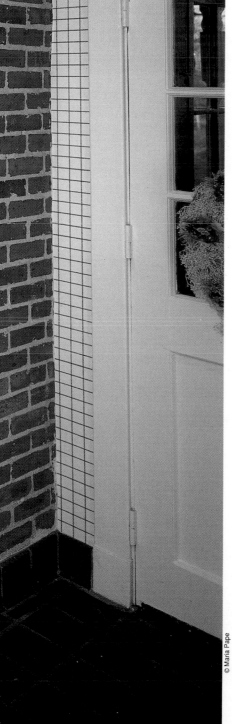

© Maria Pape

Unglazed terra cotta and natural stone require an intimate knowledge of maintenance and care procedures. In addition to stain prevention, marble and limestone have to be protected from water and vapor infiltration. An impregnator or penetrating solvent base sealer will provide the best protection for terra cotta and stone. There are many products to choose from, and each one is unique in its specifications and finish.

Once sealed correctly these terra cotta floors are practically indestructible. Over the years, they develop a rich, mellow patina which glows with a quiet fire. Small chips or scratches that might occur seem part of its texture and even enhance the overall appearance. Quickly becoming an integral part of the architecture, terra cotta flooring should last as long as the house itself.

Left: Once terra cotta tiles are installed and sealed, they generally will last a lifetime.
Below and opposite page: Two beautiful examples of terra cotta used outdoors.

AEROGRAPHY—Decorative technique developed in England, second half of the nineteenth century. Ceramic color is sprayed or blown with an air brush through a stencil onto the tile.

BISCUIT—A tile that has been fired once. Most colored glazes are applied at this stage. Tile is then fired again.

CLAY—Made of kaolin (aluminum silicate) plus quartz, sand and traces of minerals like mica, feldspar, and iron.

CUERDA SECA—Spanish decorative technique dating back to the eleventh century. Design is outlined with grooves carved into the clay to prevent running of glazes.

CUENCA—Spanish decorating technique. Designs are outlined with a raised ribbon of clay to prevent running of glazes.

DELFTWARE—Blue and white Dutch tiles. Tin glaze applied at bisque stage and then hand-painted decoration is applied.

DIE—Metal or plaster of Paris plates used to shape dust-pressed tiles.

DUST-PRESSING—A production technique invented by Englishman Richard Prosser and patented by Herbert Minton in 1840. Tiles are made from pressed dust which eliminates shrinkage. Greatly facilitated tile production and enabled tiles to be made thinner, smoother and more uniform in appearance.

ENAMEL—Ceramic color, painted on a glazed surface and then fixed by refiring at a low temperature.

ENCAUSTIC TILES— A decorative technique dating back to medieval times, used primarily for floors. Revived in second half of nineteenth century. Consists of carving out a design in the tile and filling the spaces created with a contrasting slip.

FAIENCE—Refers to the tin-glazed ceramics whose flawless glasslike transparent glaze became famous all over Europe. Name comes from the town of Faenza in Italy.

GLAZE—Silica plus metal-oxide or other colorant. At high temperatures, the silica combines with the silica in the clay body becoming part of the tile.

GREENWARE—Unglazed ceramics.

INTAGLIO—Relief in reverse.

KILN—Oven used to fire tile.

LEAD GLAZE—Glossy, transparent glaze made from lead.

LUSTER PAINTING—Decorative technique much valued by William De Morgan, English Victorian tile maker. Tile is decorated with a compound of metallic oxide. Smoke is then introduced into the kiln, reducing the

GLOS

amount of oxygen and causing the metal to precipitate out, forming a thin film of luster over the tile.

MAIOLICA TILES—Brightly colored glazes on a white opaque background of tin oxide.

MOSAICS—Small pieces of glazed tiles combined to form pictures or designs.

MOLDED TILES—Forming tiles by use of a metal or plaster die during the dust-pressing process.

NATURAL TILES—Decorative technique originated by American Low Art Tile Co. in Massachusetts in the 1870s. A real leaf or stem was impressed in the wet clay and then covered by a transparent glaze.

PORCELAIN—High-fired white clay

POUNCING—Eighteenth century decorative technique perfected by the Dutch. A design is pricked out on a paper. Charcoal dust is then rubbed over the paper, falling through the small holes to leave an outline on the tile, which is then filled in by hand.

RELIEF—Three-dimensional designs obtained by either pressing a carved wood block into the clay or pressing the clay into a box in which a design has been carved in reverse.

RESERVING—A decorative technique in which the outline of a pattern is drawn first. The background color is then painted in, resulting in a white pattern on a dark background.

SEALING WAX RED—Sixteenth century tiles produced in Istanbul. Scarlet tiles covered with a thick red glaze that stood out like a relief.

SGRAFFIATO—A decorative technique applied to greenware. The clay body is covered in a contrasting slip which is then scratched away in a pattern, to expose the underlying color.

SLIP—Liquid clay.

TIN GLAZE—A transparent lead glaze to which tin is added to make a white, opaque glaze. Useful in fixing colors painted on top of it so they do not run.

TRANSFER PAINTING—Decorative technique invented by Englishmen John Sandlere and Guy Green in the 1750s. Prints are taken from wood blocks or copper plates on thin paper using oiled ceramic color as ink. The printed paper is placed ink-side down on the tile, rubbed firmly and then soaked off, leaving the ink design.

TUBE-LINING—Victorian decorative technique. Edges of a design are outlined in slip, piped from a tube, resulting in raised lines.

UNDERGLAZE—A painted decoration under a transparent glaze.

SARY

COUNTRY FLOORS LOCATIONS

In addition to these showroom locations, Country Floors has dealers in most major cities in the United States, Canada, Australia, and Argentina.

AUSTRALIA

Country Floors
28 Moncur Street
Woollahra, Sydney
NSW 2025, Australia
(612) 326-2931

Country Floors
1256 High Street
Melbourne, VIC 3143
Australia
(613) 509-9688

CALIFORNIA

Country Floors
8735 Melrose Avenue
Los Angeles, California 90069
(310) 657-0510

Country Floors
Showplace Design Center
2 Henry Adams Street
Suite 110
San Francisco, CA 94103
(415) 241-0500

CANADA

Country Floors
321 Davenport Road
Toronto, ONT M5R 1K5
Canada
(416) 922-9214

Country Floors
5337 Rue Ferrier
Montreal, P.Q. H4P 1L9
Canada
(514) 733-7596

Country Floors
2349 Granville Street
Vancouver, B.C. V6H 3G4
(604) 739-5966

CONNECTICUT

Country Floors
12 East Putnam Avenue
Greenwich, CT 06830
(203) 862-9900

FLORIDA

Country Floors
94 NE 40th Street
Miami, Florida 33137
(305) 576-0421

Country Floors
D.C.O.T.A. Suite B-458
1855 Griffin Road
Dania, Florida 33004
(305) 925-4004

NEW YORK

Country Floors
15 East 16th Street
New York, New York 10003
(212) 627-8300

PENNSYLVANIA

Country Floors
1706 Locust Street
Philadelphia, Pennsylvania 19103
(215) 545-1040

INDEX

INDEX

INDEX